THE SMARTEST 401(k)* BOOK YOU'LL EVER READ

Maximize Your Retirement Savings . . .
the *Smart* Way!

(*Smartest 403(b) and 457(b) too!)

Daniel R. Solin

A PERIGEE BOOK

A PERIGEE BOOK
Published by the Penguin Group
Penguin Group (USA) Inc.
375 Hudson Street, New York, New York 10014, USA
Penguin Group (Canada), 90 Eglinton Avenue East, Suite 700, Toronto, Ontario M4P 2Y3, Canada
(a division of Pearson Penguin Canada Inc.)
Penguin Books Ltd., 80 Strand, London WC2R 0RL, England
Penguin Group Ireland, 25 St. Stephen's Green, Dublin 2, Ireland (a division of Penguin Books Ltd.)
Penguin Group (Australia), 250 Camberwell Road, Camberwell, Victoria 3124, Australia
(a division of Pearson Australia Group Pty. Ltd.)
Penguin Books India Pvt. Ltd., 11 Community Centre, Panchsheel Park, New Delhi—110 017, India
Penguin Group (NZ), 67 Apollo Drive, Rosedale, North Shore 0632, New Zealand
(a division of Pearson New Zealand Ltd.)
Penguin Books (South Africa) (Pty.) Ltd., 24 Sturdee Avenue, Rosebank, Johannesburg 2196,
South Africa

Penguin Books Ltd., Registered Offices: 80 Strand, London WC2R 0RL, England

While the author has made every effort to provide accurate telephone numbers and Internet addresses at the time of publication, neither the publisher nor the author assumes any responsibility for errors, or for changes that occur after publication. Further, the publisher does not have any control over and does not assume any responsibility for author or third-party websites or their content.

PRINTING HISTORY
Perigee hardcover edition/ July 2008
Perigee trade paperback edition / July 2010

Perigee trade paperback ISBN: 978-0-399-53608-3

The Library of Congress has cataloged the Perigee hardcover edition as follows:

Solin, Daniel R.
  The smartest 401(k) book you'll ever read : maximize your retirement savings—the smart way! : (smartest 403(b) and 457(b), too!) / Daniel R. Solin.
    p.   cm.
  Includes bibliographical references and index.
  ISBN-13: 978-0-399-53452-2
  1. 401(k) plans.   2. Defined contribution pension plans—United States.   3. Retirement income—United States—Planning.   I. Title.
  HD7105.45.U6S65 2008
  332.024'0145—dc22   2008006437

PRINTED IN THE UNITED STATES OF AMERICA

10   9   8   7   6   5   4   3   2   1

PUBLISHER'S NOTE: This publication is designed to provide accurate and authoritative information in regard to the subject matter covered. It is sold with the understanding that the publishers is not engaged in rendering legal, accounting, or other professional services. If you require legal advice or other expert assistance, you should seek the services of a competent professional. Continued on page 213.

Most Perigee books are available at special quantity discounts for bulk purchases for sales promotions, premiums, fund-raising, or educational use. Special books, or book excerpts, can also be created to fit specific needs. For details, write: Special Markets, Penguin Group (USA) Inc., 375 Hudson Street, New York, New York 10014.

CONTENTS

PART TWO
401(k) Plans: Rigged to Rob Your Nest Egg

PART THREE
How to Beat a Rigged 401(k) System

PART FOUR
The Care and Feeding of Your IRA

PART FIVE
403(b) Plans and Annuities—They Make 401(k) Plans Look Good!

PART SIX
Alternatives to Traditional Retirement Plans

PART SEVEN
The Closing Argument

Navigating the 401(k) Minefield

I wish I could accuse Congress of merely dithering on much needed 401(k) reform. The reality is that nothing on the regulatory horizon will address the core problems of a broken and corrupt system.

It's actually getting worse since this book was first published in June 2008. Because of the stock market crash, the average 401(k) plan participant had less money in her plan at the end of 2008 ($45,000) than she did in 1998! And she didn't have much then—only $47,000.

By some estimates, more than 33 million retirees are in danger of living their retirement in poverty. Whether these retirees and others to follow will be able to rely on Social Security and Medicare is unclear. Both programs are vastly underfunded. Social Security is underfunded by $10 trillion and Medicare is facing shortfalls between $65 and $85 trillion. These are scary numbers.

The 401(k) System Is Still Fundamentally Flawed

All of the problems with 401(k) plans I noted in mid-2008 remain unchanged. They continue to be a giant skimming operation, where brokers and mutual funds act in concert with employers to deprive employees of market returns that are theirs for the taking.

Most employers still sell out the best interest of their employees, by taking what amounts to a payoff from brokers who agree to "subsidize" the administrative costs of the plan. In exchange for their "free" plan, employers agree to let brokers select the investment options available to plan participants. No good can come of such an arrangement and none does.

The broker has hit the lottery. In exchange for paying for the administrative costs of the plan, he gets a monopoly on selecting the mutual funds for the plan. How does he make this selection? He accepts "revenue-sharing" payments from mutual funds. Those funds that pay get into the plan. Those that don't are shut out. More than 90 percent of plan advisors take these kickbacks, which are rarely disclosed.

What kind of mutual funds participate in this scheme? "Actively managed" (I call them "hyperactively managed") funds, which attempt to beat a designated benchmark, like the S&P 500. Typically, low-cost, outperforming index funds will not pay revenue-sharing. The leader in low-cost index funds, Vanguard, falls into this category. According to its director for institutional sales, "when brokers realize they won't be compensated for placing our funds in a plan, they will typically hang up on us."

Some of the abuses are really striking. Most mutual funds have two classes of shares: investor shares and institutional shares. The only difference is the cost charged by the fund family for operating each share class, which is deducted from investors' returns. Institutional shares typically require a higher minimum investment of $500,000 or more. These shares charge less than investor shares, which have far lower minimums. Lower fees are directly correlated with higher returns.

While most individuals cannot meet the minimum required to purchase institutional shares, many 401(k) plans can do so by aggregating the purchases of plan participants.

The savings to plan participants can be significant. For example, in a class action against Wal-Mart's 401(k) plan sponsor, the plaintiff alleged that Wal-Mart cost plan participants $60 million in unnecessary expenses over a six-year period by not insisting on institutional shares rather than investor shares of the mutual funds in Wal-Mart's 401(k) plan.

Everyone Wins . . . but Employees

Everyone's a winner in this cozy, secretive system—except employees. They are frequently deprived of access to low-cost, higher-returning index funds. Their plans have much higher costs than plans where no subsidies or revenue-sharing payments are paid.

The consequences of high costs can be devastating. According to the Department of Labor, a 1 percent difference in costs can reduce your account balance at retirement by a whopping 28 percent.

Don't expect your employer to take the rowing oar in reducing plan expenses. Remember, the plan is "free" to them. One study estimated that 78 percent of plan sponsors did not even know their plan costs. Why should they care? You are paying these costs.

Rome Burns While Congress Dithers

Clearly, this is a system ripe for regulation. So what is Congress doing to curb the excesses that will likely cause millions of retirees to spend their "golden years" in poverty?

Not much.

A modest proposal to simply require mutual funds to disclose all fees is bogged down in the Ways and Means Committee.

There is some effort to insure that employees get advice free of conflicts, but the details remain to be worked out.

There are 64 million reasons why a wholesale reform of the 401(k) system will not occur. According to the Center for Responsive Politics, in 2008 the securities and investment industry spent more than $64 million to have teams of lobbyists pressure members of Congress to enact legislation that would further *its* interests. As one of my colleagues noted: "The securities industry has equity in Congress."

Don't expect Congress to stop the 401(k) gravy train. The congressional cavalry is not coming.

Real Reform Is So Easy Even Congress Could Do It

Advisors to both individuals and especially to 401(k) plans have a sacred trust. They should be required to act solely in the best interest of those they serve, free of *any* conflict of interest. This legal duty (called a "fiduciary" duty) requires advisors to exhibit the highest form of trust and fidelity and to always act in their clients' best interest.

Millions of employees rely on the advice provided by advisors to 401(k) plans. Surely, these advisors must be "fiduciaries." Right?

You might think so, but how can a broker or insurance company that pays off an employer to get the coveted advisor position, and takes payoffs from mutual funds that want to be included in the plan, be a fiduciary? This conduct is clearly in *its* best interest and *not* in the best interest of plan participants.

Here's where some very clever lawyering comes in.

The Employee Retirement Income Security Act of 1974 governs the legal obligation of advisors to a 401(k) plan. Under ERISA, an employer has a legal obligation to select and monitor the investment options in a plan. The employer must select investments with costs that are reasonable and in the best interest of plan participants.

An employer can satisfy this obligation by retaining an advisor who assumes the responsibility for selecting and monitoring the investment options in the plan. If the advisor selects high-cost options that cannot be justified, the advisor has legal liability for this conduct.

Most brokers and insurance companies will not accept fiduciary liability. They provide in their Investment Management Agreements that they merely "advise" the employer concerning the investment options that will go into the plan, even though the reality is they actually make the investment decisions.

If Congress really wanted to reform the 401(k) system, it would simply require all advisors to 401(k) plans to be legally responsible to insure that the investment options in a 401(k) plan are in the best interests of plan participants. Even without regulation, employers who truly have the best interest of the employees in mind should insist that advisors to their 401(k) plans confirm in writing that they accept this responsibility. After all, isn't that why they are getting paid?

How refreshing would that be?

No bribes to get the business.

No payments to include mutual funds as investment options in the plan.

No conflicts at all between the interest of the advisors to the plan and the plan participants.

It's so easy, even Congress could do it!

An Action Plan for Employees

For 2010, the contribution limit to a 401(k) is $16,500. A plan may permit participants who are age 50 or over at the end of the calendar year to make an additional "catch-up" contribution of $5,500.

But what good is the ability to make these contributions if you have a second-rate 401(k) plan?

Setting up a first-class 401(k) plan that places the interest of the employees first is not rocket science. As indicated in Chapter 30, the government did it with the Thrift Savings Plan (tsp.gov), which is the megabillion-dollar 401(k) plan for government employees. While not every plan has the economy of scale that can drive costs down to the modest costs of this plan, much could be done to reduce the excessive costs common in most plans.

Here's an action plan for employees with 401(k) plans:

1. If your employer no longer matches, consider not participating in your plan. Instead, check out a Roth IRA to see if you qualify. If not, consider a traditional IRA and a low-cost, after-tax account.

2. If your employer matches, ask your HR department if the advisor to the plan is a "3(38) ERISA fiduciary." If not, ask why not?

3. Send the HR department a copy of the opinion of the Eighth Circuit Court of Appeals in *Braden v. Wal-Mart*. You can find it at www.ca8 .uscourts.gov/opndir/09/11/083798P.pdf. It will be a much-needed wake-up call. Your employer may not understand that your interests are not the plan administrator's first consideration, but it is likely to be *very* concerned about the possibility of legal liability for the way it has selected investment options in its 401(k) plan.

4. Check out brightscope.com. It's a new site that rates more than fifteen thousand 401(k) plans. See how your plan compares to others in your peer group. If it rates poorly, send this information to your HR department and lobby for a better plan.

5. Select investments in your plan with the goal of getting as close as possible to a globally diversified portfolio of low-cost index funds, in an asset allocation appropriate for you. This can be difficult given the poor investment choices in most 401(k) plans. Use the information in Chapter 24 as your guide.

Since the market crash of 2008, a lot of nonsense has been written about the "failure" of diversification and whether "buy and hold is dead." Don't believe any of it. John Bogle, the founder of Vanguard, recently noted, "I would just say very simply, of all the stupid ideas, the idea that buy and hold investing is dead is [the most] ridiculous." Bogle went on to note that "buy and hold" refers to buying and holding the entire stock and bond market, in an asset allocation appropriate for your age. It does not refer to buying and holding individual stocks, which he stated "has been dead forever."

Investing is not for the short term or for the faint of heart. If you have less than five years before you'll need a significant portion of your investment, you should be exposed to *no* stock market risk. Zero. None.

Diversification and buy and hold worked just as they are supposed do during the recent turbulent markets. If you invested at the peak of the market in October 2007 in the Moderate High Risk portfolio of stock and bond index funds I recommend, your portfolio lost less than 10 percent of its value at the end of 2009. Compare those returns to the returns of most investors.

Don't believe the hype that hyperactively managed funds outperform the indexes in a bear market. According to a report prepared by Standard & Poor's, more than 70 percent of all actively managed U.S. stock mutual funds underperformed their benchmarks for the five-year period ending 2008. Standard & Poor's concluded that the "belief that bear markets favor active management is a myth."

I have updated the Risk and Return Summary in Appendix B to reflect returns through 2009. This long-term data provides additional support for "Smart Investing."

In both your personal and 401(k) investing (if you can), stick to an investing plan that is validated by eighty years of historical data and hundreds of peer-reviewed academic articles.

Progress on the 403(b) Front

403(b) plans are tax-deferred retirement plans available for employees of public schools, some tax-exempt organizations, and some members of the clergy. (See Chapters 37 and 38.)

For 2010, the contribution limit for both 403(b) plans is $16,500. If you are age 50 or older, you can contribute an additional $5,500.

Regulations adopted by the Internal Revenue Service in 2007, effective

January 1, 2009, make many 403(b) plans subject to ERISA (governmental plans and certain church plan sponsors are excluded). The plan sponsor of an ERISA-covered plan must act in the sole interest of the participants of the plan. It is subject to the same requirements as plan sponsors of 401(k) plans.

These regulations significantly increase protection to plan participants. Advisors to the plan must be selected solely on the basis of demonstrable merit. Investments in the plan must be adequately diversified, unless the employee is in charge of her own investments (which the employee should insure are diversified). Most significantly, the plan fiduciary is responsible for the selection and monitoring of investment options available to plan participants.

Whether or not a plan is covered by ERISA, benefit plan attorneys are counseling their clients to act as if ERISA did apply. This is only prudent since state statutes or the common law may impose such obligations in any event.

However, as we have seen with 401(k) plans, the fact that a plan is governed by ERISA, or ERISA-like fiduciary standards, far from insures plans with investment options that are really in the best interest of plan participants.

You're on Your Own

It's unlikely that Congress is going to come to the rescue and mandate plans that truly serve the best interests of employees. This country was founded based on rugged individualism, which is premised on independence and self-reliance. Now that you understand no one will help you, and your retirement plan can be a curse as well as a blessing, you can take control of your finances and reap the fruits of your labors.

You deserve nothing less.

Daniel R. Solin
February 1, 2010

PART ONE

Rules for
All Investments

CHAPTER 1

The Amazing Story of Wan Ba-shi

In every moment of our existence, we are in that field of all possibilities where we have access to an infinity of choices.
—Deepak Chopra

There was an illusionist, Wan Ba-shi, from a remote region of China who was able to perform an amazing trick.

According to legend, he would go to a local farm and select the fattest pig from the feeding trough. He would throw an old blanket over the pig. A burst of smoke would momentarily obscure the blanket-covered pig from view. When the smoke cleared, he triumphantly pulled the blanket off the pig, and a white swan appeared in its place. Needless to say, the villagers watched in awe each time Wan performed this trick.

Fame and fortune ensued as word of his exploits spread throughout the land. Wan died at the age of ninety-eight on his expansive pig farm with many servants. He never disclosed the secret of his great illusion.

I made that up . . .

But a pig-to-swan-like conversion is precisely what is needed by many of the 70 million employees who have 401(k) and 403(b) plans.

These retirement savings plans that most Americans rely on for a financially secure future aren't set up to help employees. If you're counting on your 401(k) or 403(b) plan to safely usher you into old age, you're likely to be bitterly disappointed.

Who does benefit from these plans? Employers, insurance companies, brokers, consultants, and the mutual fund industry.

The principal culprit is the financial industry that's supposed to *help* us. Rather than leading us to financial security, the industry has placed its own economic interests ahead of those it's supposed to serve. (In the chapters ahead I'll show you just how the financial industry feeds off people planning for retirement—many of whom will end up with little more than their Social Security checks to comfort them.)

When you invest outside of these plans, you have a shot at doing so intelligently, if you follow a few basic rules.

Investing within these plans is another story. Most of them *prevent* you from making intelligent investment choices by restricting your investment options to a dizzying array of expensive, underperforming, hyperactively managed mutual funds and overpriced annuities.

You can't intelligently invest your retirement assets unless you understand some basic rules.

These rules apply to both your nonretirement assets and your retirement assets, whether you have a 401(k) plan, a 403(b) plan, a 457(b) plan, a traditional IRA, or a Roth IRA. Once you understand them, you can figure out how to best invest your retirement assets within the unfair constraints imposed on you.

Smart Investing is *not* complicated. It's actually very simple. *You* have the power to make meaningful changes to your retirement savings plan—changes that could mean the difference between retiring with dignity and barely scraping by.

You can maximize your retirement savings by learning how to avoid the minefields planted by the securities and insurance industries to explode your nest egg.

Let's start the process of converting your pig of a plan into the swan you deserve.

What's the Point?

- You can make your retirement plan work for you.

CHAPTER 2

Small Change Can Break the Bank

It will come as no surprise to anyone who has seriously
studied investment returns . . . that cost matters. In fact, the
funds in the group with the lowest expense ratios had the
highest net returns.

—John C. Bogle, "Common Sense on Mutual Funds"

If you only remember one cardinal rule about investing, this is it:
Lower costs directly relate to higher returns.

Let's start by comparing the costs of different types of mutual
funds.

What do I mean by "costs"? I'm referring to the expenses an investor is charged by a mutual fund—the percentage of a fund's assets that
investors pay to offset the expense of running the fund. This is the
cost of the fund.

High expense ratios are bad. Low expense ratios are good.

I focus on mutual funds because, as you will see, mutual funds are
the investment of choice for most investors in both retirement and
nonretirement accounts.

If your child earned a 98 percent on his math test, you'd probably be thrilled. And what if he earned a 96 percent? You wouldn't be any less happy—an A is an A.

Such a tiny difference won't matter if you're a fourth-grader, but these seemingly inconsequential percentage-point differences can make a *tremendous* difference to just about anybody who invests. A 2-percentage-point difference in expense—even 1 percent or less in a portfolio—can seriously deplete your assets over time.

Here's a simple example.

A young college graduate begins investing $200 a month in mutual funds until she retires forty years later. She earns an 8 percent annual return (before expenses) on this money, and her mutual fund of choice charges her 2 percent annually in expenses for all those many years. At the end of the line, she walks away with $400,290.

That may look respectable, but check out what she would've earned if she had put the cash in a mutual fund at a fraction of the cost—let's say 0.3 percent, an expense ratio similar to what is charged by many *index* mutual funds. If she'd done that and obtained the same returns, which is likely, her account would be worth $644,484.

Yet if someone tried to sell the typical investor a mutual fund that costs 2 percent of the investment versus 0.3 percent, most people would consider the difference to be about as inconsequential as the change you get back from a McDonald's Happy Meal.

But it's not inconsequential. That small percentage difference can make a huge impact on your retirement savings.

And the more money you've got squirreled away, the more painful a voracious fund's incisors will be. Suppose someone has $1 million in assets parked in a portfolio that earns that 8 percent annual return but chews up 2 percent of its value every year in expenses. The investor feeds another $1,000 into the account each month for twenty years. At the end, the account balance would be $3,774,556. Nice, right?

But wait: If our millionaire had invested in funds with expenses kept at 0.3 percent, the ending balance (again, assuming the same returns) would be $5,212,877.

That's a stunning difference of $1,438,321!

And he earned this without having to work on weekends or make any other financial sacrifices. He just had to pick a dirt-cheap index fund.

These possibilities make the investment world break out in hives. The people who sell stocks, bonds, mutual funds, and annuities would rather we all invest blindfolded, oblivious to the huge differences that costs make in our portfolios, because these higher costs provide them with higher commissions.

And it is fairly easy for them to get away with this charade. After all, aren't we conditioned to believe that the more expensive the product, the better it is?

The industry doesn't want to let us in on its biggest secret: Expensive mutual funds usually perform *worse* over the long term than less expensive, comparably invested ones.

Perhaps this is why investors don't receive bills that clearly set forth the cost of their investments. Can you remember ever opening an annual invoice from your mutual fund company? Do you get a bill for your variable annuity? Do you get a statement explaining just how much you *really* paid for those municipal bonds?

Of course not.

What the mutual fund industry shares with us about our expenses is miserably inadequate. What each fund does provide, by law, is a hypothetical scenario in its semiannual reports. If you flip through the document, you won't find your actual expenses: You'll find a chart that shows what a *potential* $1,000 investment would cost in expenses *if* the fund generated a 5 percent return.

This reliance on cookie-cutter hypotheticals is obviously silly. Every fund company could easily provide the *exact* amount its customers spend annually in expenses. Some consumer advocates have demanded—unsuccessfully—that the government mandate this personalized disclosure. Whether the government will ever do so remains to be seen . . . but don't hold your breath.

What's the Point?

- Focus on the expense ratios of your mutual funds—they'll make a huge difference in your returns.

CHAPTER 3

Passive Is Aggressive

*The deeper one delves, the worse things
look for actively managed funds.*
—William Bernstein, *The Intelligent Asset Allocator*

L et's define some basic terms.

"Actively managed" funds strive for investment returns that are better than a target market benchmark, like the Standard & Poor's 500 index, by researching and trading individual stocks or bonds.

"Index funds" (sometimes referred to as "passively managed" funds) simply track market averages—and make no effort to beat them—by buying and holding the securities in their target indexes.

Which type of fund do you choose? Do you try to beat the markets by purchasing actively managed funds? Or do you buy index funds that are virtually *guaranteed* to equal market returns (reduced by the low expenses of these funds)?

Here's where the amount of the expenses you're paying on your portfolio becomes important. The average actively managed fund has an expense ratio of 1.50 percent. The average index fund has an expense ratio of only 0.25 percent.

This significant difference in cost is the primary reason why index funds almost *always* outperform actively managed funds over the long term.

People who study the capital markets for a living don't seriously debate whether "active" or "passive" management is better. Rex Sinquefield, cofounder of Dimensional Fund Advisors, summarized it this way: "So who still believes markets don't work? Apparently it is only the North Koreans, the Cubans and the active managers."

The financial press tells quite a different story. Unfortunately, the daily media grist of hype and hysteria that promotes certain stocks and actively managed mutual funds influences many investors.

Here's a glaring example:

Money magazine called Bill Miller, who manages the Legg Mason Value Trust Mutual Fund, the "iconic fund manager of his generation." Others have pegged him as "one of the greatest investors of our time," who is not only "brilliant" but also "legendary."

What did Miller do to deserve this fawning? For fifteen years in a row, Miller's actively managed fund beat its benchmark, the Standard & Poor's 500-stock index.

The *real* story didn't make the headlines: For those fifteen years, no other mutual fund manager matched Miller's winning streak. Not one!

The financial industry's marketing machines portray portfolio managers as savvy financial pros, but in reality, they routinely slip on banana peels.

These managers are allowed to invest in *any* promising stock or bond within their official mandate. A manager like Miller, whose fund is devoted to large companies, can sink his money into any blue chips he covets.

Active fund managers can avoid whatever they wish, too. During the 2007 subprime mortgage meltdown, Countrywide Financial Corporation, the country's largest mortgage lender, plummeted to its lowest stock price in nearly four years in just a few nightmarish days. An active fund manager could have ditched Countrywide Financial in a heartbeat (although few did).

In contrast, the rules for the guys operating index funds are practically draconian. The indexers must track their benchmarks as closely as possible. For instance, an index fund that's tied to the Standard & Poor's 500-stock index must invest in all 500 blue chips in the benchmark. So when the '07 mortgage meltdown hit, the large-cap (large companies that the market values at over $10 billion) index fund managers had to hold their noses and keep their shares of Countrywide Financial because the mortgage lender belongs to the S&P 500 index.

Similarly, when the notorious Enron was sinking, the indexers had to own the stinker, while the actively managed counterparts were free to shed their shares.

Given all this, actively managed stock pickers must have a huge advantage over index funds, right?

Then how was it that only *one* active fund manager—out of thousands—beat the S&P 500 for fifteen years?

In reality, it's the indexers, with their rigid rules, who typically triumph in the long term.

A lot of investors assume they'll simply pick the active funds that have recently soared to the top of the charts. That's a flawed strategy, because past performance is like looking in a rearview mirror. We can identify previous winners, but there's no reason to believe that those funds will continue to do well. In fact, the opposite is true: Relatively few funds that perform well in one year are able to repeat that stellar performance in the following year.

The death count for actively managed funds is quite high, but you wouldn't necessarily know it. The fund industry covers up its mistakes by merging them with better-performing funds. According to Standard & Poor's, 29.3 percent of actively managed domestic stock funds were either shut down or merged during the last five years—almost one-third. When bad mutual funds die along with their dreadful records, the rest look better than they actually are.

You'd think that the active managers' dismal performance would scare off investors, but no. Most investors are still invested in actively managed mutual funds. So it's only natural that they continue to make this mistake when selecting investments for their retirement accounts.

And by the way, Bill Miller's sterling record turned to mush after his impressive streak ended. By the end of 2007, the three-year annualized returns of the flagship fund he managed were 3.64 percentage points *below* the S&P 500. Even worse, his 2007 record was horrendous. His fund was the worst performer among all comparable funds tracked by Lipper, a highly respected mutual fund research firm.

You can't help it if others are seduced by the lure of better returns using actively managed funds. You should not be among them.

What's the Point?

- Invest in index funds.

- Ignore the hype in the financial media.

CHAPTER 4

A Simple Strategy for Superior Returns

Most of my investments are in equity-index funds.
—William F. Sharpe, Nobel Laureate in Economics, 1990

If anybody can strike it rich in Wall Street's minefields, it should be the nation's corporate pension funds. These corporate behemoths have the money to hire the best financial minds in the country.

But if you're thinking that the returns for these highly paid, highly educated stock jockeys must be incredible, you'd be wrong. In reality, these lauded investment managers can't even scale the simplest investment hurdle.

During one fifteen-year period, for instance, 91 percent of institutional money managers, who were overseeing more than two hundred major corporate pension funds, failed to outfox a simple combination of two indexes. All the managers' fancy financial moves couldn't beat a portfolio that sank 60 percent of its assets into the Standard & Poor's 500 index, which contains the nation's blue-chip stocks, and 40 percent in Lehman Brothers Aggregate Bond Index, the best-known benchmark for the bond market.

If these guys can't equal or exceed the markets, what chance do you have to achieve superior returns?

Actually, your chances are excellent. The secret to pulling this off is incredibly easy:

Simply aim for market returns using index funds.

You might hear brokers say that market returns are just "average." They're not: They're far superior to the returns achieved by the vast majority of actively managed funds.

As you now know, the humble index fund aims to do no better or worse than its benchmark. For instance, the Vanguard 500 Index Fund is linked to the Standard & Poor's 500-stock index. The S&P 500 contains the nation's best-known and biggest companies, like General Electric, Microsoft, Target, and Hershey.

I'm not suggesting that anyone hold all assets in an S&P 500 fund. That would be far too risky for most investors. (In Chapter 13, we'll discuss an appropriate asset allocation for you.) I'm using the S&P 500 index simply as an illustration of a major index that's used as a benchmark by many equity mutual funds—most of which fall short of equaling its yearly returns.

Capturing market returns starts to look more exciting when you compare it to its alternative. Morningstar, a leading provider of investment research, once examined the long-term performance of 1,446 actively managed large-cap stock funds during a decade-long period and discovered that only 35 of them matched or beat the S&P 500. That's less than 2.5 percent. A shockingly dismal record.

Historically, index fund investors have enjoyed greater returns over time than almost all actively managed mutual funds. Fixed income, or bond, index funds, as well as those that track international stocks and other investment categories, can claim the same bragging rights.

Every quarter, Standard & Poor's produces a report card that stacks index returns against actively managed funds. In the report card's most recent five-year period, the indexes beat every category of small, medium, and large stock funds.

In some categories, the whipping was particularly rough. The average mid-cap growth fund, for instance, generated a 6.61 percent annual return versus the index's 9.56 percent return. While the small-cap growth index returned an annual average of 10.95 percent for five years, the typical small-cap growth fund mustered just 6.86 percent.

Why are index funds so successful?

Costs are the biggest reason. Because index funds don't pay analysts to scour the financial data in a usually fruitless effort to "beat the markets," they're much less expensive to run. The difference in costs between actively managed funds and index funds can save you tens of thousands of dollars, or even hundreds of thousands of dollars, over your lifetime.

Indexing also succeeds because Wall Street is efficient. Stock prices reflect what's already public knowledge about a particular stock. It's tough for the MBA stock picker to outsmart his competitors. If Microsoft or Home Depot makes an announcement, the price of the stock will be adjusted within seconds. The efficient market has stacked the deck against the actively managed mutual funds.

So whatever your level of financial sophistication may be, superior returns are yours for the taking.

Grab them!

What's the Point?

- Market returns are superior returns.

CHAPTER 5

Just Because It Quacks, It May Not Be a Duck!

*Surprisingly, one-third of all index funds carry either
front-end or asset-based sales charges. Why an investor
would opt to pay a commission on an index fund when a
substantially identical fund is available without
a commission remains a mystery.*
—John C. Bogle, "Common Sense on Mutual Funds"

I've told you why index funds outperform actively managed funds, and why market returns are superior to actively managed fund returns. But don't just buy any old index fund. You want to make sure you're investing in the right ones—the low-cost ones.

Some index funds are incredibly expensive. Why? Because the wolves have snuck into the henhouse. Many mutual fund shops, irritated by the increasing popularity of indexing, have added an index fund or two to their lineup just to satisfy investors. Unfortunately, some of them have expense ratios that are much higher than comparable index funds offered by the industry leaders.

Buying the right index fund is very simple. Look for the ones with the lowest expense ratios. You can find them at the major fund families, like Vanguard, Fidelity, T. Rowe Price, and Charles Schwab. (I have no affiliation with any of these firms.)

What's the Point?

- Buy the lowest-cost index funds from one of the major fund families.

CHAPTER 6

"Hot" Advice Can Give Cold Comfort

If stock market experts were so expert, they
would be buying stock, not selling advice.
—Norman R. Augustine

Trying to pick stocks that will outperform the markets is no better
than picking actively managed funds. Both are less than zero-
sum games (because of the costs), in *and* out of retirement plans.

You'd think if anyone could pick stocks, the financial media could.
In the summer of 2000, *Fortune* magazine enthusiastically announced
the results of its exhaustive search to find the very best stocks for the
first decade of the new millennium. The staff narrowed the field to ten
golden stocks that included Charles Schwab, Oracle, Nokia, Morgan
Stanley, Univision, and, yes, Enron.

When the picks were revisited five years later, the average negative return for this motley corporate crew was roughly 50 percent . . . a
negative 50 percent! Obviously, Enron wasn't the only stinker in the
bunch.

The same is true of efforts to time the markets.

One study looked at 237 market-timing investment newsletters
(which are supposed to tell investors when to get in and when to get

out of the markets) from 1980 to 1992. Almost all of the newsletters went out of business by the end of the study. The average life of these market-timing "experts" was only four years.

The financial media pushes consumers to pick stocks and attempt to time the market. If you do, you're likely to fare as badly as *Fortune*'s readers and the readers of these newsletters, rather than enjoying high market returns.

What's the Point?

- Don't engage in stock picking or market timing.

CHAPTER 7

"Hot" Funds . . . and Other Fables

Contrary to their oft articulated goal of outperforming
the market averages, investment managers are not
beating the market; the market is beating them.

—Charles D. Ellis, "The Loser's Game,"
Financial Analysts Journal, July–August 1975

B rokers and advisors often use investment researcher Morningstar's "star" rating system to pitch hot mutual funds based on recent performance. A five-star rating means huge inflows for mutual funds. A one- or two-star rating can mean significant outflows as investors flee these funds.

Over the years, considerable research has demonstrated that high Morningstar ratings aren't predictive of future performance. Some of these studies demonstrated little difference between the performance of five-star and three-star funds in the years after the rating was given.

A recent study found that, with minor exceptions, index funds *outperformed* all of the Morningstar-rated mutual funds, including the much-hyped five-star funds.

Another study of mutual funds selected by Morningstar for its own

401(k) plan found that these funds significantly *underperformed* a broad U.S. market index for the period 1991–99. The same study found that funds designated as "top performing" by *Forbes*, the *New York Times*, *Worth* magazine, *Business Week*, and fifty-nine investment newsletters studied over a ten-year period all *underperformed* the same index.

Add picking "hot" mutual funds to your list of bad investment practices. It's just as bad as stock picking or market timing.

What's the Point?

- Don't try to pick "hot" mutual funds.

CHAPTER 8

Don't Confuse Activity
with Progress

Investors are motivated by greed and fear—not
by sound investment practices.
—"Quantitative Analysis of Investor Behavior," Dalbar Inc., 2007

The grass-is-greener syndrome is one of the reasons why we're a nation of antsy investors who can't resist channel-changing our way through our portfolios. Greed, after all, is a powerful motivator. So is fear: We'd rather bail before we get clobbered.

Overconfidence also fuels our antsiness. Plenty of investors overestimate their own prowess. Overconfidence leads to excessive trading, which leads to higher costs . . . which lead to worse returns.

Combine these psychological reasons with overzealous, commissioned brokers who push investors to make unnecessary portfolio changes, and it's no wonder it seems impossible for investors to leave their portfolios alone.

Every year Dalbar Inc., a financial services consulting firm, examines the investing behavior of Americans and documents this impatience, concluding that it seriously erodes our net worth.

Here's an example:

During the past twenty years, the Standard & Poor's 500-stock index generated an annualized yearly return of 11.8 percent. If you'd bought an S&P 500 index fund and held it for those twenty years, you would have enjoyed those same yearly returns (minus the fund's low expenses).

But during the same period, Dalbar determined that mutual fund investors captured an average yearly return of a paltry 4.3 percent.

Bondholders didn't do any better. For much of the past twenty years, long-term government bonds have enjoyed tremendous annual returns of 8.6 percent. You'd think bond investors would be thrilled, but their accounts haven't shared in the prosperity. The average fixed income investor eked out a pathetic return of 1.7 percent—because most investors didn't actually *hold* the bonds for twenty years, preferring instead to sell rather than wait for the high returns.

Why this appalling performance? Some of the blame rests on investors' fear or greed. And then there's the hubris factor. A lot of people think they know what's going to happen in the market because the financial media's talking heads say so—and they always seem so certain that they're right.

In 2003, for example, these "investment professionals" predicted that long-term interest rates, which were at lows unseen since John F. Kennedy was in the White House, had to be poised for a rebound. And when these interest rates jumped, nobody would want old bonds that offered lower interest rates than the new ones would offer, so long-term bonds would get hammered.

After hearing these confident predictions, investors dumped bonds. In fact, the holding period for bonds was only 2.6 years.

Ironically, bonds were fine that year—but you couldn't say the same for investors who took a hit because they relied on these predictions and dumped their bond holdings.

Don't confuse activity with forward motion. As one pundit said, "A rocking horse keeps moving, but does not make any progress."

What's the Point?

- Activity increases costs, which can reduce returns.

CHAPTER 9

Risky Behavior

If your broker is not familiar with the concept of
standard deviation of returns, get a new one.
—William Bernstein, *The Intelligent Asset Allocator*

It's impossible to be a Smart Investor without understanding risk.

Anybody who works in the financial industry has been asked the "magic bean question": "I'm not willing to take any risks with my money, but I want an investment that generates high returns. What do you recommend?"

I call this the magic bean question because only in fairy tales could you find risk-free investments that generate high returns. Short of running off with the giant's magic beans or finding the leprechaun's pot of gold, you're out of luck.

If you aren't willing to take risks, you can't expect to pocket impressive returns. You'll have to be content with the returns on your savings account, which will be eroded by inflation.

And the greater an investment's potential risk, the greater potential reward. The punier the risks, the punier the rewards.

Here's what I mean:

If you invest in 30-day U.S. Treasury bills, which are backed by the full faith and credit of the federal government, you face virtually no chance of losing any money. So if you hold onto the bill for 30 days, it's risk free.

The returns from U.S. Treasury bills reflect that. Since 1926, the Treasury bills have generated a yearly return of 3.72 percent. If someone had put $1 in a Treasury bill back in 1926, it would be worth $19.29 today—awfully underwhelming.

The U.S. Treasury's long-term bonds are just as safe from default risk as the Treasury bills, since the federal government isn't likely to renege on its debt. But because these bonds have a longer maturity, or life span, than U.S. Treasury bills, they can get whiplashed by interest rate gyrations, so they face more interest rate risk than Treasury bills. With an annualized return of 5.42 percent, a $1 investment in these bonds would now be worth $71.69.

The big leap in rewards happens when you move across the aisle to the stock market. If you invested $1 in blue-chip stocks since 1926, it would be worth $3,077.33 today. That pencils out to a 10.42 percent yearly return.

Of course, the reason for the nicer pop in returns is the greater risk. And that's going to look like peanuts compared to small-cap (or small-company) stocks, which have historically reigned as the sweepstakes winner. A $1 investment in small-cap stocks in the 1920s would be worth $15,922.43 today.

Am I advocating loading up exclusively in small-cap stocks? Absolutely not. That would be much too risky.

You don't need a high-risk portfolio to generate worthwhile returns—but you *do* need to think about how much risk of loss you're comfortable with in terms of your money.

As you'll see in Chapter 11, the best strategy is to mix and match different types of investments.

The chart on page 28 shows the historical returns of the major asset classes.

HISTORICAL INVESTMENT PERFORMANCE FROM 1926 THROUGH 2006

	Annualized Return	Value of $1
30-Day Treasury Bills	3.72%	$19.29
Long-Term Gov't Bonds	5.42%	$71.69
Large-Company Stocks	10.42%	$3,077.33
Small-Company Stocks	12.69%	$15,922.43

What's the Point?

- If you don't take risks, you'll only earn savings account returns.

- Your portfolio should consist of a mix of different classes of stocks and bonds.

CHAPTER 10

When Bigger Isn't Better

**Standard deviation is probably used more than
any other measure to gauge a fund's risk.**
—Morningstar.com's Interactive Classroom, Course 203:
Looking at Historical Risk, Part 1

After reading the previous chapter, you may wish that someone had placed a big bet on small-cap stocks back in 1926 and, eight decades later, presented you with the windfall.

Historical stock returns can seem so impressive that it's natural to wonder why we'd bother with bonds at all.

But boycotting bonds and throwing all your money into small-cap firecrackers is a terrible idea. To understand why, you have to understand standard deviation.

Standard deviation is a statistical measure that illustrates the volatility of small-cap stocks, junk bonds, emerging-market stocks, or any other investment. It provides the range of returns that a portfolio or an individual mutual fund has historically experienced.

As I wrote in *The Smartest Investment Book You'll Ever Read*, I look at standard deviation the way I look at the results of my blood tests: I don't need to know how the technicians came up with the numbers, but I do need to know what's healthy.

The higher the standard deviation, the riskier the investment.

Not surprisingly, when you look at standard deviations going back to 1926, the investments with the highest-octane returns also offer the scariest standard deviations. Here's a sampling:

	Historic Return	Standard Deviation
U.S. Treasury Bills	3.72%	3.1%
Long-Term Gov't Bonds	5.42%	9.2%
Large-Company Stocks	10.42%	20.08%
Small-Company Stocks	12.69%	32.74%

So what do these percentages mean? Let's take large-company stocks for an example. Since the 1920s, blue-chip stocks have averaged a yearly return of 10.42 percent, but the performance will typically (two-thirds of the time) range anywhere from a gain of 30.5 percent to a loss of 9.66 percent.

Since 1926, large-cap stocks (as measured by the S&P 500) have suffered through only one four-year period in which stocks floundered in the red—the Great Depression. In 1939 through 1941 and again in 2000 through 2002, investors suffered through losses for three consecutive years.

If small-cap or large-cap stocks scare you, remember: They won't look so menacing when they're mixed with other investments. A portfolio that only contains small-fry stocks will be intensely scary, but one that also includes large stocks, foreign and emerging-market stocks, REITs (real estate investment trusts), short-term bonds, and U.S. Treasury Inflation-Protection Securities (TIPS) won't bite nearly as hard. Adding a variety of investment categories that behave differently smooths out the ride.

The general guidelines for an appropriate standard deviation, as I outlined in *The Smartest Investment Book You'll Ever Read*, are as follows: For conservative investors, a standard deviation no higher than 8 percent; for moderately aggressive investors, no higher than 15 percent; for very aggressive investors, no higher than 20 percent. And no one's portfolio should have a standard deviation higher than 30 percent.

I suggest a model portfolio in Chapter 14 and in Appendix B. When you get to those sections, take a look at the standard deviations of those portfolios. This will give you an excellent understanding of their risk. You can then decide which one is right for you.

What's the Point?

- Standard deviation measures the risk of your portfolio.

- Make sure your portfolio's standard deviation isn't too high for your tolerance for risk.

CHAPTER 11

Lose the Empty Calories

Putting yourself on investing autopilot minimizes the
opportunities for your brain to perceive trends that
aren't there, to overreact when apparent trends turn out
to be illusions or to panic when fear is in the air.

—Jason Zweig, *Money* magazine, September 27, 2002

Do you know what you own?

If somebody took a peek at all the stuff you've got crammed into various investment accounts, would it look as disheveled as a football locker room?

Most people don't gather investments in any sort of systematic way. They collect their financial goodies based on emotions, tips, or conventional wisdom—making their portfolios about as healthy as a bucket of fried chicken.

If you want to be a successful investor, you've got to get rid of your portfolio's empty calories. And the way to do that is to intelligently and strategically diversify, using a variety of different types of investments.

The goal of diversification is to end up owning a healthy portfolio that's positioned to capture the highest financial rewards for the amount of risk you're willing to take. This might sound hard to pull off, but it's not. Adopting one of the model portfolios I describe in

Chapter 14 and Appendix B is the simplest way to implement a diversified portfolio. One of these portfolios is likely to be suitable for you.

When you diversify, you end up lessening the volatility that spooks so many investors by carefully choosing what asset classes deserve a spot in your portfolio. You're not aiming for a perfect dinner party guest list—well-behaved guests who get along. When you diversify, you're aiming to gather assets that have absolutely nothing in common. Ultimately, you want your portfolio to be the financial equivalent of yin and yang.

Disparate investments are highly desirable because they'll cushion the blow when the bond and/or the stock markets become fussy. During times of financial turbulence, it's highly unlikely that every investment category will behave the same way. So when large-cap stocks crash, for instance, chances are that short-term bonds—or another asset class in your portfolio—will be hanging tough. Diversifying offers your portfolio a greater measure of protection.

For example, in the last three-year negative period for stocks (2000–2002), the S&P 500 lost 37.61 percent. However, during that same period, an investment in the Wilshire All REIT Index had a gain of 52.54 percent. The returns from an investment in this asset class would have cushioned the losses in your large-cap stocks.

There are countless asset classes that you can use for your building blocks. A partial list includes domestic large-company stocks, small-company stocks, international stocks, emerging-market stocks, REITs, commodities, TIPS, and U.S. Treasury bonds. The various stock categories are also divided into two camps: value (a stock that investors believe is trading for less than it is worth for a variety of reasons, including the perceived undervaluation of its assets) and growth (a stock that appears attractive because of its potential growth in earnings).

Bonds are often sorted by their maturity. Short-term bonds with brief maturities are going to be less volatile than the intermediate or long-term variety because short-term bonds are more immune to interest rate changes.

When assembling broad investment categories, you can get as simple or as complicated as you'd like. You can keep it very simple by owning just three mutual funds that invest in domestic stocks, foreign stocks, and bonds. That's precisely what I recommend in my model portfolios.

What's the Point?

- Diversifying your portfolio offers protection against risk.

CHAPTER 12

The Simplest Way to Beat the "Pros"

These two new studies show that you can succeed as
a do-it-yourself investor. Not only can you do it, you
can do *better* than these paid professionals.
—Mary Dalrymple, "Beat the Pros," *The Motley Fool*, December 27, 2006

In order to intelligently invest in your retirement portfolios, you first need to figure out how to do so outside of those portfolios. This is the easy part, because you have no constraints on what investments you can choose.

Here's how to do it. You'll hold investments in a group of funds that, in turn, have investments in all the securities (stocks or bonds) in a particular index. This portfolio is very easy to implement.

You will hold investments in funds that represent three broad indexes:

1. An index fund representative of the U.S. stock market in its broadest terms;

2. An index fund representative of the international stock market in its broadest terms; and

3. An index fund representative of the U.S. bond market in its broadest terms.

In order to implement the right portfolio for you, you need to follow this simple, four-step process:

1. Decide on your asset allocation.

2. Open an account directly with a respected company, such as Vanguard, Fidelity, or T. Rowe Price.

3. Invest the stock and bond portions of your portfolio in low-cost index funds from the fund family you select.

4. Review your portfolio once or twice a year to determine whether it is necessary to rebalance it in order for it to remain aligned with your original asset allocation or support a new asset allocation that meets your changed investment objectives and/or risk tolerance.

In the following chapters, I will take you through each of these steps.

What's the Point?

- Implement your nonretirement portfolio with three low-cost index funds.

CHAPTER 13

Your Biggest Investment Decision Takes Only Fifteen Minutes

Investment policy [asset allocation] is not only the
most important contributor to performance—it is
even more important than originally thought.
—Roger J. Surz, Dale Stevens, and Mark Wimer, "Investment Policy
Explains All," *Journal of Performance Measurement*, Summer 1999

Asset allocation is the division of an investment portfolio among three types of investments—stocks, bonds, and cash equivalents like Treasury bills or certificates of deposit. Asset allocation is the *one* big decision you need to make.

Research shows that asset allocation accounts for 90 percent or more of the variability of your returns. The specific securities held in the portfolio (stock picking) accounts for about 5 percent, and market timing accounts for a mere 2 percent.

To determine your optimal asset allocation, you should consider:

- Your age

- Your risk tolerance

- Your health

- Whether or not you need income from your portfolio

- Changing life events (divorce, death of a spouse, loss of a job)

I've included a questionnaire to determine the asset allocation that's appropriate for you (see Appendix A). It'll take about fifteen minutes to fill out.

For an even easier way to do this, go to www.smartestinvestment book.com. You'll find an interactive version of the questionnaire, with automatic calculations.

There are many other questionnaires available online, including an excellent one by Index Funds Advisors at www.ifa.com (with whom I am affiliated).

Now you should have a suitable asset allocation. The most difficult—and critical—part of this process is done.

By the way, when was the last time your broker or advisor called and said, "I want to talk about your asset allocation"?

What's the Point?

- When constructing a portfolio, nothing is more important than your asset allocation.

CHAPTER 14

Simple Investing Is Smart Investing

I have often said . . . that any pension fund manager who
doesn't have the vast majority—and I mean 70 percent or
80 percent of his or her portfolio—in passive investments
is guilty of malfeasance, nonfeasance or some other kind
of bad feasance! There's just no sense for most of them
to have anything but a passive investment policy.
—Merton Miller, Nobel Laureate in Economics, 1990

I've prepared model portfolios using index funds managed by Vanguard, Fidelity, and T. Rowe Price. I've included the Vanguard portfolio here; you can find all of the portfolios in Appendix B. They're very easy to follow and tell you precisely which funds to select and what percentage of your portfolio should be invested in each fund, depending on your asset allocation.

One of these portfolios will work for the vast majority of investors.

For each of these portfolios, take the total amount of the assets you will be investing in stock funds, and invest 70 percent of that amount in a domestic stock fund and 30 percent of that amount in an international stock fund. There is strong academic evidence that portfolios with some exposure to foreign markets have similar historical returns—*with less risk*—than portfolios invested only in the domestic stock market.

COMPOSITION OF FOUR VANGUARD MODEL PORTFOLIOS

Fund Name	Low Risk	Medium-Low Risk	Medium-High Risk	High Risk
Total Stock Market Index Fund (*VTSMX*)	14%	28%	42%	56%
Total International Stock Index Fund (*VGTSX*)	6%	12%	18%	24%
Total Bond Market Index Fund (*VBMFX*)	80%	60%	40%	20%
	100%	100%	100%	100%

If you decide to open an account with Vanguard, just do the following:

- Invest 70 percent of your stock allocation in the Vanguard Total Stock Market Index Fund Investor Shares (VTSMX).

- Invest the remainder of your stock allocation (30 percent) in the Vanguard Total International Stock Index Fund (VGTSX).

- Invest 100 percent of your bond allocation in the Vanguard Total Bond Market Index Fund Investor Shares (VBMFX).

If you want more detailed information, I've included a comprehensive chart in Appendix B that shows the risk and return data for these portfolios for a thirty-eight-year period. However, even when you are considering long-term data, it is important to remember that investing still involves risks. There may be long periods of time when you will not realize the average annual returns of the various portfolios set forth in Appendix B.

In order to have a reasonable prospect of achieving these returns, you should be prepared to hold the low-risk portfolio for four or five years, the medium-low-risk portfolio for six or seven years, the medium-high-risk portfolio for eight or nine years, and the high-risk portfolio for ten or more years.

If you do not anticipate being able to hold your portfolio for a minimum of four or five years, or if the thought of *any* loss in a given year frightens you, you should consider the "ultra conservative" portfolio, which consists solely of six-month Treasury bills. You can purchase them directly from the U.S. Department of Treasury by going to www .treasurydirect.gov.

While a portfolio of Treasury bills will expose you to very little risk of loss, you need to be aware that interest must be reported as income on your federal tax return in the year the Treasury bill matures. The interest is exempt from state and local taxes. In addition, the returns from Treasury notes may not keep pace with inflation, thereby exposing you to what is known as "inflation risk."

We're almost done with basic investing principles!

What's the Point?

- Pick the model portfolio that's right for you.

CHAPTER 15

DFA's Way (or the Highway)

The reverence DFA enjoys among many of the advisors who
use its funds is legendary. Listen to true believers talk and
it wouldn't require a leap of faith to imagine that if God were
an investor, Heaven would use DFA funds exclusively.
—Bloomberg, *Wealth Manager* magazine, November 2002

s it possible to improve on the returns you could get from retail
low-cost index funds without trying to pick stocks or "beat" the
market?

The answer may be yes—by investing in a portfolio of institutional index mutual funds from Dimensional Fund Advisors (DFA).
DFA funds track their own Dimensional Indexes, which are designed
not only as benchmarks, like most other well-known indexes, but as
investment vehicles.

DFA has come up with a way to maximize the possibility that
investors in its funds have a better investing experience. It makes its
funds available through approved fee-only advisors who have demonstrated their knowledge of DFA funds. DFA has found that the use
of a professional advisor helps avoid erratic investor behavior that
can end up being extremely counterproductive to a portfolio. Investor
behavior has been shown to be a major factor in preventing investors
from achieving success with their investments, according to studies by

Dalbar, Morningstar, and *Money* magazine. (Full disclosure: I invest in DFA funds for my own portfolio; I recommend DFA funds to my individual and institutional clients; and I also recommend them for inclusion in 401(k) plans. I receive no compensation, directly or indirectly, from DFA for doing so.)

DFA-approved advisors are required to screen clients who wish to invest in DFA funds and to construct for them a "buy-and-hold" globally diversified portfolio of DFA funds. Rebalancing the portfolio over time is recommended to maintain the proper risk level.

Think of DFA's institutional index funds as Vanguard index funds on steroids. Like Vanguard and other low-cost index fund managers, DFA's funds have custom indexes, low transaction costs, and low turnover. DFA does not engage in stock picking, market timing, or forecasting of any kind.

The key to DFA's success lies in its ability to create better indexes designed to capture the excess returns historically found with small and value stocks. While a traditional small-cap index fund that tracks the Russell 2000 index has to kick out its small-cap stocks when these little guys outgrow the benchmark, DFA creates its own construction and trading rules that allow for patient trading strategies in order to achieve lower costs and increase returns for its shareholders. In addition, the stocks in DFA's funds typically have smaller market capitalization and are more value tilted than the stocks in its peer index funds. Stronger tilts toward value and small stocks—for which DFA is best known—are key. Academic research by Eugene Fama and Kenneth French has repeatedly shown that value and small stocks have historically rewarded investors with significantly greater returns. DFA, which has two Nobel laureates on its board of directors, bases its investment strategy strictly on academic studies.

DFA is fixated on trying to squeeze as much return as possible out of its wide assortment of global large- and small-value stocks. This strategy has paid off for its investors. During the past decade, the

Dimensional U.S. Small Cap Value fund has generated an annualized return of more than 12.5 percent, which places it in the top 6 percent of funds in that category. Its five-year record of 20.8 percent puts it among the top 3 percent of its peers.

An increasing number of investors and retirement plans are concluding that, after all fees, DFA's investment approach, coupled with a passive investment advisor, creates a powerful combination. DFA currently manages more than $150 billion in assets from both institutional investors and advisor-guided individuals.

A recent study validated these views. It compared comparable portfolios of DFA passively managed funds and Vanguard index funds and found that the DFA portfolios significantly outperformed the Vanguard portfolios during the period studied. Of course, there is no assurance that this stellar past performance will continue in the future.

Finally, there is compelling data supporting the decision of DFA to make its funds available only through advisors who take the time to fully educate their clients on DFA's investment philosophy. A study from Morningstar showed that over a ten-year period the *actual* returns achieved by DFA investors exceeded the returns earned by investors in other no-load index mutual funds by a whopping 3.74 percent a year.

DFA also offers its funds through 401(k) plans. Unfortunately, DFA funds are rarely included as an option in these plans because DFA does not offer "revenue-sharing" payments to brokers or advisors as an inducement for them to recommend its funds. In addition, DFA is not well-known to many plan administrators since it does no advertising.

Investors who are using a 529 plan to fund higher-education expenses can access DFA funds. West Virginia offers a Smart529 Select plan that features age-based portfolios consisting solely of DFA funds. You just pick from one of the seven portfolios designated with the age range of your child.

Ask your company benefits office to do its due diligence on DFA and to determine if employees would be better served by a 401(k) plan that included DFA's institutional index funds rather than the more expensive and poorer performing hyperactively managed retail funds that dominate most plans. We'll be discussing 401(k) plans in depth later.

What's the Point?

- DFA funds may be a suitable option for investors in their personal portfolios and retirement plans.

CHAPTER 16

Keep Your Balance
by Rebalancing

**Left free to drift, a portfolio can evolve into one with an asset mix that
has decidedly different risk and return characteristics than intended.**
—Dan Goldie, financial advisor

As you've learned, asset allocation is crucial. But your investments in both stocks and bonds can drift away from your initial
asset allocation.

For instance, a 60/40 stock-to-bond allocation could be 45/55 stock-
to-bond after six months if the value of stocks falls dramatically, or
75/25 if the value of stocks rises dramatically. Every six months or
so you'll want to check your portfolio to determine if rebalancing is
appropriate.

Rebalancing can also be necessary when a life event—a health scare,
a career move—has changed how much of your portfolio's income you
might need, or your sense of how much risk you can assume.

When you rebalance, don't be tempted to ride the winning asset
class. It's difficult to sell some stocks, put the proceeds into bonds,
and then watch the remaining stock portion of your portfolio go even
higher. That will happen many times. However, no one knows what
the future holds. If you end up having too much stock exposure when

stocks tank, you'll incur greater losses than what you might be willing to comfortably tolerate. Selling your winners and buying the losers— it's a prudent way to keep your portfolio in good shape, but it's a very hard thing to have the discipline to do.

There are two ways to rebalance your portfolio.

If you have an opportunity to add new money to your portfolio, you can buy more of the assets that have fallen below your asset allocation plan.

If you can work only with your current assets, you'll need to sell some of the assets that are overrepresented in your portfolio, and buy more of the assets that are underrepresented.

If you use an investment advisor, he should contact you every six months or so to go over your portfolio and see if there is any reason to change your asset allocation, then perform the necessary transactions for you to rebalance. If the advisor doesn't call, make the call yourself.

Remember that there may be tax consequences when rebalancing in taxable accounts. You will need to take this into consideration.

A number of firms, including Vanguard, have established model portfolios for retirement investments that automatically rebalance at regular intervals. Vanguard calls these funds Vanguard Target Retirement Funds. These funds have different asset allocations, depending on your "target" retirement date. The target funds use mostly Vanguard index funds, including those I recommend.

So if you don't want to do your own rebalancing, you can simply invest your retirement savings in one of the Vanguard target funds. Other major fund families have target funds as well, but be careful. Many of them have actively managed funds in them. I would not recommend any Target Retirement Fund that is not made up mostly of index funds.

I'll discuss the benefits of Target Retirement Funds in more detail when we talk about the options that should be available (and usually aren't!) within *all* retirement plans. They are a salve for most of the woes that afflict investors who want to maximize their retirement savings the Smart Investor way.

That's it! You now know how to invest your nonretirement assets. It should be just as easy to invest your retirement assets.

Unfortunately, it isn't. But the same basic principles can serve as your guide.

What's the Point?

- Consider the necessity of rebalancing to keep your asset allocation intact.

PART TWO

401(k) Plans:
Rigged to Rob Your
Nest Egg

CHAPTER 17

Can You Feel Guilty Without a Conscience?

It's starting to look like 401(k) plans will go down in history as a costly failure. In fact, the abandonment of old-fashioned pension plans is likely to leave many Americans poorer in their old age.
—K. C. Swanson, TheStreet.com, April 8, 2002

First, some history.

In 1980, a Philadelphia-area bank president asked Ted Benna, a consultant, to create a plan that would scrap its annual cash bonuses and require its employees to hold on to the money until they stopped working at the bank.

Why rile up so many working stiffs by holding out on their eagerly anticipated annual bonus? Economics, of course. The bank's president wanted to capture a tax break by creating some sort of deferred profit-sharing plan. But he also envisioned a retirement plan that would keep it competitive with other area banks.

Benna found a new section of the Internal Revenue Code, entitled 401(k). By relying on this section, Benna created a plan that would permit employees to put pretax money into a tax-deferred account. This plan was revolutionary, since many large employers had savings plans that only allowed workers to contribute after-tax money.

When the bank rejected the idea, Benna set up what's thought to be the nation's first 401(k) plan at his own consulting firm.

America's blue-chip companies quickly adopted 401(k) plans when they realized that they are far cheaper (for the company!) than traditional pension plans (which guarantee retirees monthly checks for life). With traditional plans, employers were paying almost 90 percent of the pension costs for these employees.

So while the 401(k) exploded out of nowhere, the nation's traditional pension plan system turned into a shrinking violet. Today, more than 653,000 401(k)-type plans exist throughout the country, and the contribution of employers has been reduced to less than 50 percent. The aggregate savings to employers has been estimated to be in the "hundreds of billions" of dollars.

During the 401(k)'s infancy, more than 148,000 traditional pension plans existed, but today less than 47,000 are left standing. Since 2001, the number of *Fortune* 1000 corporations that have frozen or shut down their pension plans has more than tripled.

Cost wasn't the only attraction. With pensions, companies must assume all the risks—the big one being that there will be enough money in the kitty to honor their obligations. But with 401(k) plans, employees are standing in front of the bull's-eye all by themselves. They have to make all the investment decisions, kick in a significant amount of money, *and* assume the killer risk of inflation.

What a deal!

Once you understand this history, you start to appreciate that the primary beneficiary of 401(k) plans is the employer. The securities and insurance industries are the secondary beneficiaries. Guess where you come in?

Think caboose.

But many companies are still not satisfied. In order to reduce their costs even further, they have essentially sold out their employees and made it difficult for you to invest successfully for retirement.

In the next few chapters, you'll understand how greed has rigged the system against you—and what you can do about it.

What's the Point?

- 401(k) plans were intended to benefit employers, not employees.

- Your 401(k) plan transfers all the financial risk to you.

CHAPTER 18

Knowledge Is Power

**When advisors are conflicted and hidden financial dealings determine
which managers are hired, ultimately pension performance suffers.**
—Ed Siedle, securities attorney

Imagine walking into the men's department at your favorite store
and being greeted by a salesman who has an ulterior motive. He is
secretly paid a fatter commission when he successfully cajoles customers into buying a specific designer's suits.

After the salesman fusses over you, you walk out of the store with a
double-breasted suit that doesn't quite fit and seems dated—and you
wonder why you bought it.

If a sartorial double-cross would upset you, imagine how you'd feel
if financial-industry insiders were conniving to get your boss to pick
completely inappropriate 401(k) funds for you and your colleagues.

This happens all the time.

Highly compensated consultants are quietly paid to steer companies into picking expensive, underperforming funds for inclusion in
401(k) plans. Very few people, including many employers, know this.

Almost every major corporate employer relies on the services of
these consultants to help select 401(k) investment options, as well as
the investments for traditional pension plans. There are almost two
thousand consultants in this field. They're supposed to place the inter-

ests of the employees above their own and give objective, transparent advice that's free from conflict.

Unfortunately, for many pension consultants, this simply isn't the case.

Many pension advisors offer "free" administrative services to employers in exchange for selecting their 401(k) funds.

And what funds do they select? Often they're expensive, hyperactively managed funds that have historically *underperformed* low-cost index funds over the long term.

Why do you think they choose these?

Because these funds "revenue share" with them. "Revenue sharing" is a nice term for an ugly practice: The advisors are paid by the funds they select to be included in your 401(k) plan.

Do you think revenue sharing might influence the decision of the "objective" advisor to put these funds in your 401(k) plan?

Of course! And it gets worse.

Many pension advisors have "consulting relationships" with both employers *and* the mutual funds they recommend for inclusion in the plan.

So much for disinterested, objective advice!

What's the Point?

- Advisors with conflicts of interest may not place your interests first.

- The funds in your plan may not be there based on merit alone.

CHAPTER 19

So Many Fees, So Little Time

Most participants continue to operate under the false notion that their 401(k) is "free." That's a myth.
—McHenry Revenue Sharing Report, "Revenue Sharing in the 401(k) Marketplace: Whose Money Is It?"

The expenses related to any investment are a big deal. The same goes for the costs associated with 401(k) plans.

However, the numbers involved with 401(k) plans are staggering. By some estimates, excessive 401(k) fees will cost you as much as *20 percent* of your retirement assets.

When the cost of gas inches up another five cents, most of us notice. Grocery stores are so aware of their shoppers' price sensitivity that many post signs above the lettuce when the price jumps suddenly.

But you can't get outraged about price if you don't know what you're paying.

That's one of the reasons why millions of people who sink money into their 401(k) plans are getting gouged—big-time.

Why don't you know what you're paying? Because you're not given an accounting of these fees. You probably assume that the "professionals" who manage the plan have your best interests at heart. Unfortunately, they don't.

In addition, many employees have no idea they're getting ripped off because they think that their 401(k) is "free." Employees often assume that their employers are paying for the retirement plans, but that's not true.

Who picks up the 401(k) tab? In most cases, you do.

Nearly 50 million workers are paying fees for 401(k) plans that their employers select. Since the workers are footing the bill, employers don't have to be aggressive about managing expenses. Hey, it's not the company's retirement that's at stake! It's yours.

It would be bad enough if workplaces were simply foisting off the hidden costs onto their employees. But in many cases, employers are *intentionally* selecting plans that are studded with killer expenses. Still other companies are inadvertently choosing plans with dreadful costs without understanding what they've done.

Either way, the effect is disastrous. The retirement dreams of millions of Americans are being jeopardized because few people are going to complain about something they can't see and don't understand.

A major reason why 401(k) costs are invisible is how they're sold. Most 401(k) plans today are bundled and lump together administrative fees and expenses charged by the funds in the plan. In a typical scenario, a 401(k) vendor—a mutual fund firm, a brokerage house, an insurance company, or even a solitary stockbroker—will propose plans with different lineups of mutual funds. Some plans will require the company to kick in money for record keeping and other overhead costs. But many companies gravitate to plans that will cost them very little or nothing for these services.

If the executives who choose a company's 401(k) plan asked, they'd discover why their plans are so terrible: The plans are stuffed with mutual funds that gouge the workers with Porky Pig fees. These fees generate so much cash that there's more than enough to pay for the overhead costs that the employer normally covers.

So even during the 401(k) search process, the worker bees' desire to build up a fat nest egg collides with the employers' goals of cutting costs.

Employees would be far better off if companies selected plans that contained inexpensive index funds or Exchange Traded Funds (index funds that trade like stocks on major stock exchanges, known as ETFs) or, better yet, passively managed funds from DFA. But most index funds, ETFs, and passively managed funds are low cost and don't "revenue share," so including them would require the company to kick in some cash to cover the overhead.

Some 401(k) plans charge expenses as high as 2 to 4 percent. Among the most outrageous plans are those that contain annuities peddled by insurance companies and brokerage firms. Most of these are found in the 401(k) plans of small companies. I discuss annuities in more detail in Chapters 39 through 43 in the context of 403(b) plans, where the misuse of these investment products is epidemic. But don't skip that section just because you don't have a 403(b) plan. Annuities are completely inappropriate investments for most people, and you'll need this valuable information to protect yourself against aggressive annuity salespeople.

What are employees getting for these gigantic fees? Certainly not superior performance. Quite the contrary: All the academic evidence proves that low-cost index funds will outperform expensive, hyperactively managed funds (and annuities) over the long term.

Obviously, the primary beneficiaries of these high fees are the mutual funds who charge them. No wonder the mutual fund industry is one of the world's most profitable, earning an estimated pretax profit of 30 percent or more annually.

Whether you're paying 3 percent or 0.5 percent might not seem like a big deal at first—but remember our discussion of the vast difference a seemingly small percentage change can make?

Let's suppose, for instance, that a husband and wife invested a total of $12,000 annually in his-and-her 401(k) plans that generated annual returns of 9 percent (before expenses) over a working career of thirty-five years.

If they poured money into their plans that charged 3 percent, they'd walk away with $1.42 million before taxes. Sounds good! But if they'd invested in a plan with minuscule expenses of 0.5 percent, their take-home amount would pencil out at $2.51 million before taxes.

The difference: *$1.09 million!*

What's the Point?

- High expenses and poor investment choices can gut your 401(k) returns.

CHAPTER 20

Company Stock: The Nail in the 401(k) Coffin

Company stock is a sideshow for the vast majority of people who work for a living. Including company stock in any 401(k) plan turns a prudent, diversified investing program into a lottery.
—Scott Burns, columnist, *The Dallas Morning News*, March 17, 2002

A few years back the trade publication *Pensions & Investments* published a survey that startled even those of us who are already cynical about corporate America.

The survey looked at America's biggest companies to see what percentage of their corporate 401(k) or 401(k)-like retirement plans contained company stock. The results were mind-boggling. Most of the cash in the retirement plans of some of the nation's biggest blue chips was sunk into company stock. At some corporations, more than 80 percent or even 90 percent of the cash was tied up in company stock—an incredibly dangerous amount.

We all grumble about our jobs, but as investors, too many of us are far too loyal to our employers.

Investing in the stock of your employer is "stock picking." Individual stocks are extremely volatile, and the odds are stacked against those who try to pick "stock winners."

What comes to mind when you start thinking about the downside of worker loyalty? Enron, of course. Enron workers had close to 58 percent of their money sunk into that corporate scallywag when its stock dropped nearly 99 percent.

But you don't need Enron's cataclysmic meltdown to illustrate why you should stay away from your company's stock in your retirement plan.

For starters, familiarity incorrectly breeds confidence. Too many employees think that because they work for a company, they're well aware of the financial status of that company. And it's dangerous for an employee whose paycheck depends on a company's performance to also put her retirement in the hands of that company.

Your investment position is way too concentrated—and, therefore, risky. If anything happens to the company, you not only lose your livelihood: You also lose your retirement nest egg.

Sure, there are examples of those who struck it rich on one stock. But you're way more likely to sabotage your retirement if you make one big stock bet.

Even respectable companies can experience rough patches that wreak havoc on a portfolio. During the 1990s—that go-go period of unbelievable stock gains—the company stock of Toys "R" Us managed a worse-than-anemic yearly return of –5 percent. Large corporations like Hilton Hotels, Dole Foods, Kmart, and JCPenney didn't fare much better.

Corporate America likes employees to invest in stock because it promotes loyalty, and the company gets to pocket tax breaks. Unfortunately, some employers force their workers to invest in their stock because they insist on using stock for matching 401(k) contributions.

Employees, however, are fighting back. Employees of such corporations as Pfizer, Kodak, AIG, Lucent, Enron, and Citigroup have sued after dramatic drops in their company-stock values.

If you're voluntarily investing in company stock, stop doing it. If you have your company's match stuck in its stock, see if you can liberate the cash and move to better and more diversified 401(k) choices.

There are much better places to invest that money.

What's the Point?

- "Enrons" can happen when you least expect them.

- Don't invest a large percentage of your 401(k) plan funds in company stock.

CHAPTER 21

If It's Broken, Fix It!

When the boomers retire between 2010 and 2030, most will find the cupboard bare. The inevitable government bailout will make the savings and loan resolution of the last decade look like lunch at Taco Bell. The 401(k) is likely to turn out to be a defined-chaos retirement plan.

—William Bernstein, "Riding for a Fall," *Barron's*, November 26, 2001

Unfortunately, 401(k) plan results are the most unfavorable for the employees who can least afford them—those at the lowest end of the salary scale.

In one study, workers in the top fifth of compensation had 401(k) returns that were on average *500 percent higher* than those in the bottom fifth. There's a very good chance that these less fortunate employees will retire in poverty.

But that's not all.

There's strong evidence that 401(k) plans as a whole underperform the markets. In one particularly startling example, the returns of 401(k) plans of five leading financial firms (Morningstar, Prudential, Hewitt, Citigroup, and Merrill Lynch) were compared with the S&P 500 and other benchmarks over the period from 1995 to 1998.

The 401(k) plans of all of these financial firms significantly underperformed both the S&P 500 and a basic index of 60 percent stocks and 40 percent bonds.

How could this happen?

According to a prominent consultant, "The administration of many 401(k) plans reflects a culture in which high costs are hidden and poor performance ignored."

The combined loss to you and fellow employees as a consequence of the mismanagement of your 401(k) plans is estimated to be "in the trillions."

Let this be your wake-up call.

Now let's discuss what you can do to protect yourself from a 401(k) system that is rigged to plunder your nest egg.

What's the Point?

- The current 401(k) system is a disaster waiting to happen.

PART THREE

How to Beat a Rigged 401(k) System

CHAPTER 22

Why Fifteen Is Your Magic Number

A central premise of 401(k) plans is employee choice, and at each step of the way, too many workers are making choices detrimental to their long-term wealth—choices that threaten not just a comfortable retirement, but the ability to fund even a basic standard of living.

—John Bogle, author and founder of the Vanguard Group

How much money should you tuck away during your career?

A study conducted by Barclays Global Investors, the world's largest provider of indexed investments, tried to answer that question. It found that the typical 401(k) savings rate is 8 to 9 percent, including the employer's match.

What happens if a worker saved 9 percent for forty years and earned 3 percent yearly salary increases? The study found that after all expenses were deducted, the worker would enjoy a 6 percent annual return.

That means that if the employee faithfully kept this up for forty years, he would be able to replace only *41 percent* of his preretirement income!

With Social Security benefits, maybe you could retire on that income. However, the study noted that this assumed no unemployment, no borrowing from the plan assets, no taxable distributions during the life of the plan, and a decent rate of return. These calculations did not take into account inflation. The authors accurately described these assumptions as "heroic."

Clearly, this is not a plan that should give you comfort.

So, what should your savings goal be?

Here is the chilling conclusion of this study:

How much would this worker have to save to replace the 75% of pre-retirement income that is often considered the benchmark for a successful retirement? A 15% savings rate is about right for medium to high income employees, again given 40 years to save, with no borrowing or preretirement payout, if the investor can earn a decent realized return—"decent" meaning the market rate of return on a medium-risk portfolio that is on the efficient frontier [an optimal portfolio that has the highest expected return possible for the given amount of risk], minus index-fund-level fees. Since almost no one gets this many lucky breaks, the savings rate had better be much higher than 15% in periods when the participant *can* save.

Now that you know the *minimum* amount you should be saving, let's see how you compare to the millions of Americans with 401(k) accounts.

Each year the Employee Benefit Research Institute, a nonprofit public policy research organization, and the Investment Company Institute, the trade organization for the mutual fund industry, release a report card on how well we're faring as retirement savers.

The data is not encouraging: The average worker's 401(k) balance is only $61,346.

But even this figure is misleading because the average is pulled up by some very large accounts. A more realistic figure is the median 401(k) account balance, which looks at the point where the balances of half of the accounts are above this amount and the balances of half of the accounts are below this amount.

The median 401(k) account is only $18,986.

This means that 50 percent of all accounts are worth no more than $19,000. Chances are you're closer to having $19,000 in your account than the $61,000 "average." At this level the picture looks extremely depressing for the majority of plan participants.

Saving anything is better than nothing, of course. Many Americans save nothing. About 27 percent of eligible workers ignore their 401(k) plans entirely. Unless they have made alternative arrangements to save for their retirement, they are courting disaster.

Here's the bottom line: Unless you both significantly increase the percentage of your income that you are saving for retirement and change the way you invest your 401(k) assets, your retirement will not be the "golden years" of your dreams.

What's the Point?

- A *minimum* savings rate of 15 percent, including your employer's match, is critical for a successful retirement. But you need to be a Smart Investor.

CHAPTER 23

Smart Investing in a Dumb Plan

On average, 90 percent of the variability of returns and 100 percent
of the absolute level of return is explained by asset allocation.
—Roger G. Ibbotson and Paul D. Kaplan, "Does Asset Allocation
Policy Explain 40, 90, 100 Percent of Performance?"
December 1998, revised April 1999

Now that you know how much you should be saving—at least 15 percent of your income—let's discuss how to invest that amount. The latest 401(k) figures show that Americans would be richer if they spent more time figuring out into which investment cubbyholes they should be putting their 401(k) cash.

The primary reason for dismal returns is poor asset allocation: Not enough money is invested in stock mutual funds, which historically have higher returns than other investment options.

Of course, it doesn't help that most 401(k) plans are "dumb plans." They offer a bevy of high-expense-ratio, underperforming, hyperactively managed mutual funds and precious few low-expense-ratio index funds, ETFs, and passively managed funds.

The typical twenty-something only invests 50.4 percent of his or her account in stock mutual funds. That's awfully low for investors that age, considering that their timeline could be forty years or more.

Thirty- and forty-somethings are also too timid with their stock allocation. The typical worker in his or her forties invests only 54.3 percent in stock funds.

What those numbers don't show is how skittish people are about investing in *any* stock funds within their 401(k) plans. Here's the breakdown:

Age Group	Percentage Not Invested in *Any* Stock Funds
20s	47.0%
30s	32.7%
40s	31.4%
50s	34.2%
60s	41.8%

It doesn't matter how old you are: Even people on the verge of retirement should be invested in stock mutual funds to some extent.

Why?

Well, life doesn't stop when you leave your retirement party. You could still have thirty or more years left of sleeping in every morning. And only stocks will help you fight one of your pesky retirement demons—inflation.

The asset allocation questionnaire in Appendix A will give you a good idea of the amount of your 401(k) assets that should be invested in stock mutual funds.

What's the Point?

- Determine the maximum amount you should invest in stock mutual funds.

CHAPTER 24

Beat a Rigged System

I now believe that if an investor is to buy only one U.S.
index fund, the best general U.S. index to emulate is the
broader Wilshire 5000 Stock Index—not the S&P 500.

—Burton G. Malkiel, *A Random Walk Down Wall Street*

Ideally, every 401(k) plan would be stuffed with low-cost index funds or ETFs or passively managed funds and Target Retirement Funds (where the underlying funds were index funds). If you had these options, your portfolio would likely perform better than 90 percent of all professionally managed money over the long term.

But what if your 401(k) plan doesn't include these choices? In that case, try to get as *close* to an ideal portfolio as you can.

Though you should lobby for better choices in your 401(k) options, here's what you can do now: Search for funds in your plan that behave the most like index funds.

Here's the only cheat sheet you'll need to do that. It's a list of alternative mutual funds that substitute for index funds.

To be included in this list, a fund had to contain at least $500 million in assets and charge below-average expenses. Some of the funds, however, assess a sales commission, which is unfortunately true of too many funds in 401(k) plans.

The funds that survived this screening—included on the list below—most closely resemble these three index funds:

- Vanguard Total Stock Market Index Fund (VTSMX)

- Vanguard Total International Stock Index Fund (VGTSX)

- Vanguard Total Bond Market Index Fund (VBMFX)

Why these funds? Because, as I said in Chapter 12, if you invest in this trio, you'll be covered in all the necessary investment categories.

The Domestic Stock Fund list below includes funds that act like the Vanguard Total Stock Market Index Fund. This fund contains large, medium, and small companies, and is a quick way to get exposure to the Wilshire 5000, which includes most domestic stocks.

The second list, International Stock Funds, correlates to Vanguard's Total International Stock Index Fund.

The Bond Funds list includes funds that resemble Vanguard's Total Bond Market Index Fund, which invests in a broad index of high-quality domestic bonds.

Look at the three categories: Is there an index fund in each that's offered through your 401(k)?

If so, that's the fund you should work with.

If your 401(k) includes more than one fund in each list, pick the one with the lowest expense ratio.

If you have a choice, consider avoiding the funds that hit you with a sales charge.

Domestic Stock Funds	Expense Ratio (2007)
American Century Equity Growth Inv.	0.67%
Evergreen Large Cap Equity I	0.91%
Fidelity Disciplined Equity	0.92%

Domestic Stock Funds	Expense Ratio (2007)
Fidelity Stock Selector	0.88%
Franklin Templeton Core All Equity A	1.40%
Goldman Sachs Strategic U.S. Equity	1.15%
Hartford Disciplined Equity HLS IA	0.72%
ING VP Growth & Income	0.59%
Mainstay MAP A	1.33%
New Covenant Growth	1.34%
Northern Growth Equity	1.14%
Oppenheimer Main Opportunity A	1.08%
Pacific Cap Growth & Income A	1.53%
Principal Inv SAM S/G A	1.39%
Putnam Investors A	1.08%
RiverSource Large Equity A	1.06%
Russell Diversified Equity S	0.98%
SA U.S. Market	1.18%
Schroder N. American Equity Inv.	0.33%
Schwab 1000	0.34%
T. Rowe Price Spectrum Growth	0.96%
Thornburg Value A	1.35%

International Stock Funds	Expense Ratio (2007)
Fidelity Overseas	1.00%
Guidestone Int'l Equity GS4	1.30%
Hartford Int'l Opportunity HLS IA	0.75%
MFS Research Int'l A	1.46%
Russell Int'l Securities S	1.22%
Vanguard Int'l Growth	0.55%

Bond Funds	Expense Ratio (2007)
Baird Aggregate Bond Inst.	0.30%
Diversified Core Bond Inv.	0.96%

DWS Core Fixed Income Ins.	0.62%
Evergreen Core Bond I	0.55%
Goldman Sachs Core Fixed Income A	0.84%
ING Intermediate Bond A	0.69%
JP Morgan Core Plus Bond S	0.69%
Managers Fremont Bond	0.79%
Pimco Total Return A	0.90%
Putnam Income A	1.05%

Your goal is to get as close as possible to the model portfolio option that you chose from the model portfolios listed in Chapter 14 and Appendix B.

What's the Point?

- If your 401(k) plan doesn't offer an appropriate selection of index funds, try to find a comparable mutual fund.

CHAPTER 25

Cheat the Cheaters
with an IRA

**For many retirees, the money won't be there and this will have
a direct effect on most Americans' standard of living.**
—J. Carter Beese Jr., former SEC commissioner

Millions of people are stuffing money into 401(k) plans that offer investment choices as appealing as stale Fritos. The typical 401(k) lineup is often a mishmash of mediocre and expensive funds that don't even cover the basics.

For instance, your company's 401(k) might include three funds that all invest in large-cap stocks—but there isn't a single small-company stock fund in the bunch. Your 401(k) might offer a junk bond fund—but no international stock fund. I'm sure you get the picture.

I've given you some options for how to work around the constraints of your 401(k), but here's another idea: Reduce your dependence on your 401(k) by investing in an individual retirement account (IRA). Sometimes these accounts are also known as individual retirement arrangements.

With an IRA—a savings plan that provides income-tax advantages to people saving money for retirement—you can fill in the gaps left wide open by your 401(k), and no one can force you to sink money into any investment that you don't want. (We'll be discussing IRAs more in Part Four.)

How should you go about this?

One option is to open an IRA and invest some of the money that you normally would have tucked inside a 401(k). (IRA contributions are limited to a certain annual amount—currently $5,000 a year for investors under fifty, and $6,000 a year for those fifty and over.)

If your employer refuses to provide a match for your 401(k) contribution, switching your allegiance to an IRA is an easy decision. Employer matches aren't princely, but you shouldn't snub them: Typically, employers kick in 50 cents for every dollar employees invest, up to 6 percent of pay. So if you make $50,000 and contribute 6 percent of your salary, you would invest $3,000 in the 401(k) and place any other investment money into an IRA, up to the maximum allowed contribution.

Here's another IRA strategy: Select investments for your IRA to compensate for the weakest, or missing, links in your 401(k).

This will be easier if you step back and think of all your retirement holdings as sitting in one big pot—rather than trying to figure out how to invest in a 401(k) and then repeating the process with your IRA, a spouse's IRA, and any other retirement accounts.

By now you know that your asset allocation—*how much should be in stocks versus bonds—is the most critical investment decision you can make.* You also know that 30 percent of your stock assets should be in an international stock index fund and the balance should be in a broad domestic stock index fund that uses the Wilshire 5000 as its benchmark.

Here's an example of how this strategy might work.

Suppose your 401(k) has only one hyperactively managed, international mutual fund. You believe you'd be better off with a low-cost international index fund.

Consider doing this:

Invest the bond and domestic portion of your stock portfolio in the funds available in your 401(k) plan.

Invest the amount allocated to international stocks in a fund through your (or your spouse's) IRA.

Why? Because IRAs allow you to invest in just about anything you could possibly want. In this case, the Vanguard Total International Stock Index Fund would be an excellent choice.

When deciding which assets belong in your IRA or other retirement accounts, and which ones should go into regular taxable accounts, there is another factor to consider.

Bonds generate ordinary income that is taxed at ordinary income rates. Stocks (if held for more than one year) will generate capital gains that may be taxed at the lower long-term capital gains rates.

To the extent possible, you should try to put bonds in tax-deferred or tax-free accounts (like your 401(k), an IRA, or a Roth IRA, which we'll discuss in Chapter 35) and put stocks in taxable accounts. This allocation will permit you to maximize the tax benefits of your retirement accounts.

When you finish with this process, the portfolios in your 401(k) and IRA accounts might look lopsided individually—but remember to look at the big picture. What's critical are the overall percentages of those key investment categories across all your retirement and nonretirement accounts.

Taking time to mix and match investments might seem like a hassle—but it's definitely worth it.

What's the Point?

- Consider using an IRA to get better investment choices than those offered in your 401(k) plan.

- Consider your retirement and nonretirement accounts as one investment pot.

CHAPTER 26

When Cashing In Is Cashing Out

A projected 40 percent of today's baby boomers are likely to depend
almost completely on Social Security's poverty-level benefit
after age 70, just as today's lower-income seniors do today.
—Testimony of Michael Calabrese before the Subcommittee on Health,
Employment, Labor & Pensions, Committee on Education and Labor,
November 8, 2007

Imagine for a minute that you're on the verge of quitting your job. You're excited, since you're leaving behind a boss whose ego is bigger than Donald Trump's and your next work space won't be the size of a shower stall.

As you're packing up, you think: Why not cash out my 401(k)? After all, you could use the money. So you arrange to take it with you, and you head out the door.

When you reach your car, a masked guy with a gun demands that you hand him your wallet—with all that 401(k) cash.

This may seem preposterous, but it happens every day . . . without the masked guy or the gun.

Many American workers rob their own 401(k) accounts of obscene amounts of money without giving it much thought. They kill their nest egg by cashing it out.

According to Hewitt Associates, which conducts regular surveys of 401(k) behavior, *45 percent* of people leaving a job empty their workplace account. For workers in their twenties, it's nearly 66 percent who cash out.

Most people don't see the consequences of cashing out a 401(k) until later: The stickup is subtle. They conclude that the amount they'll pay in fees—your employer will withhold 20 percent of your 401(k) account's value for taxes—is worth it to gain access to that money.

But that 20 percent is just the down payment.

Here's why:

The Internal Revenue Service will see all that liberated 401(k) cash as income. So you'll owe income taxes on the amount—and, if your state has its own income tax, you'll get smacked around a second time.

Many people will also get slammed by a nasty penalty. If you're less than 59½ years old, you'll typically have to pay a 10 percent penalty for pilfering your 401(k) account.

When you add up the taxes and penalty, you can see how you may as well have been robbed at gunpoint.

Let's say that you're in the 25 percent tax bracket when you left your workplace with a 401(k) that's worth $100,000. Now assume that cashing it in will bump you up to the 28 percent tax bracket. Besides the federal bill, you will end up paying 9 percent in state taxes as well as the early withdrawal penalty. Add all that up, and you'll ultimately lose $47,000.

The fees can be even more excruciating if you've borrowed against your 401(k). When you quit your job, you're expected to repay the loan promptly. If you can't, the government will consider the loan's outstanding balance a withdrawal, subject to taxes and that potential penalty.

Instead of cashing out, consider these options:

- Roll the money into an IRA.

- Roll the money into a new 401(k) plan.

- Leave the money in the existing plan.

For the vast majority of employees, any of these options will be preferable to cashing out your IRA.

What's the Point?

- Cashing out your 401(k) rarely makes sense.

CHAPTER 27

The Trick to Transferring Company Stock

The average person doesn't have a shot at understanding this.

—Mark Cortazzo, senior partner with MACRO Consulting Group

Y ou should now have tattooed on your brain what *not* to do with your 401(k) when you retire or leave your job.

But what about your company stock that you may be holding within your 401(k) plan? I believe employees would be wise to avoid holding company stock in their 401(k) plans, but there are many reasons why you might not have been able to follow this advice.

If you do have company stock, the care and feeding instructions for this part of your 401(k) are different. And counterintuitive.

You might assume the best place for highly appreciated company stock is inside an individual retirement account or other tax-deferred account, but it's not.

A better option might be to usher the stock into a taxable account and pay taxes and, if applicable, an early withdrawal penalty. That's the counterintuitive part.

Here's why: If you move your stock shares into a traditional IRA, you'll be taxed at your income tax rate when you withdraw the money during retirement—which could be as high as 35 percent based on current rates, or even higher if income tax rates go up.

The tax hit will be considerably smaller if you segregate the company stock into a taxable account, where you'll only pay up-front taxes on the cost basis (the amount that you paid for the stock over the years, or the value of the stock on the date your employer contributed it to your account, if you received company stock as part of a matching contribution), which you can obtain from your employer.

Here's what I mean: Say you paid an average of $15 a share for your company stock over the years. Now it's worth $150 a share. If you move it to a taxable account, you won't incur taxes on the $135-a-share profit, called the net unrealized appreciation, until you actually sell it, which could be years later.

When you do pay the tax, you will pay the maximum long-term capital gains tax rate, which is currently just 15 percent.

The 10 percent early withdrawal penalty might make you pause—but it's not as bad as you might think.

Usually, departing workers under 59½ must pay the penalty if they don't keep their 401(k) assets in a retirement account. There are some exceptions to this rule. For example, you would not have to pay the 10 percent additional tax if you received the distribution after you left the company and you left the company during or after the calendar year in which you reached age 55 and your departure from the company qualifies as a separation from service.

But even if you have to pay a penalty, it could be puny if you paid relatively little for the stock. That's because the penalty is based on the stock cost basis, *not* on what it's worth today.

Suppose your stock is worth $70,000, but the cost basis is just $7,000. The early withdrawal penalty would be $700—not $7,000.

Let's look at how these two alternatives play out:

You leave your company with 1,000 shares of company stock that you purchased at different prices over the years. Today's share price is $50, so today your stock is worth $50,000. The cost basis, however, is just $10,000.

You're in the 35 percent tax bracket, and you rolled the stock and everything else in your 401(k) into an IRA. Years later, you sell the stock in your IRA for $75,000 and withdraw these funds. The federal tax bite, based on your tax bracket, would be $26,250 (assuming current tax rates).

In contrast, if you had stuck those stock shares in a taxable account when you quit your job, you would have paid an income tax of $3,500 and a $1,000 penalty, both based on the cost basis.

But when you sold the stock, your profit ($65,000) would have been taxed at the vastly preferable long-term capital gains rate of 15 percent. You'd have paid $9,750. When you add that to the tax and early withdrawal penalty you paid earlier ($4,500), your total bill would have been $14,250.

That's a lot better than $26,250.

One caveat: By holding on to your company stock, you are increasing your risk. If this is an issue, you could consider transferring your company stock into an IRA, selling it, and diversifying your portfolio. While the tax hit may ultimately be less beneficial, the reduction in risk may be worth the trade-off.

What's the Point?

- Consider transferring company stock in your 401(k) into a taxable account and taking the tax hit instead of transferring the stock to an IRA.

CHAPTER 28

Can a Fox Advise
the Chickens?

**If we don't start doing a better job of managing the nation's
retirement wealth, in another ten or fifteen years, we
could be facing a social crisis that dwarves the Great
Depression in terms of magnitude and duration.**
—Donald Trone, founder of the Center for Fiduciary Studies, August 2007

If you break your arm, would a doctor ask you to set the bones yourself? If your car needs a new transmission, will your mechanic hand
you the wrench?

Of course not. But if you're saving money in a 401(k), you're expected
to know what you're doing. You're supposed to be a financial whiz,
even if you're lousy at math and you've never picked up a copy of the
Wall Street Journal—or you just don't have the time to figure it out.

Employers know this is a ludicrous assumption, but traditionally
their response has been: Tough luck.

With pensions disappearing, you're expected not only to shoulder
the burden of saving for your retirement but also to assume the duties
of investment portfolio manager.

Why don't employers do more to help? Typically, it's because they're
worried about giving investment advice—they're paranoid that some

disgruntled guy in the mailroom who lost money in the stock market might sue them.

Now, things are changing. Thanks to the landmark federal Pension Protection Act of 2006, employers are encouraged to provide counseling through fiduciary advisors, who will discuss investment goals with individual workers.

But just because the advisor sitting across from you was hired by your company doesn't mean you should trust him with your financial future.

In September 2007 the Harvard School of Business and the University of Oregon released a devastating study that made stockbrokers and advisors look like a bunch of bozos.

In the study, the highly credentialed authors examined the performance of thousands of broker-sold mutual funds, comparing them to the funds that individual investors buy on their own.

The "professionals" kicked butt, right?

Wrong!

Let's look at some of the numbers:

The individual investors earned a yearly return of 10.54 percent for their stock funds during the period from 1996 to 2004.

The brokers' clients? They mustered a yearly return of 8.04 percent.

The study found a similarly gaping difference in foreign fund investments: the little guys' 9.2 percent return versus the 7.74 percent return the clients of financial pros earned. What's even more incredible is that brokers underperformed the Average Joe investors even *before* their sales charges were deducted.

Why did the brokers lag so badly?

Because these advisors are often more interested in their own welfare than their clients'. They appeared to select funds based on the size of their fees and not on what was best for the people who trusted them. What's more, brokers were guilty of the same destructive behavior as so many individuals—chasing hot returns.

So why should *anyone* pay large brokers' fees for inferior returns when they can do much better themselves?

Investors wrongly assume that the guys sitting in the corner offices know what they're doing. If more investors compared their mutual funds to the appropriate benchmarks, a lot of brokers would get bounced.

What's even more troubling is that investors often don't even understand the standard of care their broker owes them. They know the name on the business card, but often that's about it.

Many people don't even know if the guy providing them advice is a broker. That's because the brokerage industry has succeeded in erasing the distinctions between brokers, who are simply salesmen, and registered investment advisors. You'll never spot the term "stockbroker" on a business card today. Instead, you'll see "wealth manager," "financial consultant," and "retirement specialist."

Misleading titles matter: They mask a major peril in using stockbrokers. A broker's first loyalty is to the employer, whether that be Merrill Lynch, UBS, Smith Barney, or any of the lesser-known brokerage firms. A broker can sell stocks to a client that his firm is eager to peddle, or he can push particular mutual funds and annuities that will financially benefit the firm.

In most of their dealings with their clients, brokers aren't considered fiduciaries. In its simplest terms, a fiduciary puts his clients' interests first. He can't foist a mutual fund on a client because someone else will benefit. There can't be any ulterior motives. Fiduciaries must always act in the very best interests of their clients.

In the next chapter we'll discuss how to find a competent advisor.

What's the Point?

- Don't assume that brokers add value.

- You may be the best advisor you will find.

CHAPTER 29

Beware of "Financial Professionals" Bearing Gifts

More money is lost in the stock market than in legal and illegal casino gambling combined.

—Marvin Steinberg, PhD, a Connecticut psychologist who specializes in treating compulsive investment gamblers

Many investors can very competently handle their own financial affairs by following the simple guidelines in this book. They don't need any advice.

For those of you who do, be careful. The financial field is rife with impostors. Almost anyone can call himself a "financial expert." Beauticians face higher certification hurdles than financial advisors.

To avoid hiring someone who spews financial nonsense, search in the right place. Begin by looking for a registered investment advisor (RIA). RIAs must register with either the U.S. Securities and Exchange Commission or their state (if they manage less than $25 million).

These advisors must agree to be fiduciaries, which means they must put their clients' welfare before their own. An RIA, for example, can't recommend that an elderly couple get a deferred variable annuity, because it wouldn't be in their best interest. (You'll see why when we discuss annuities.) Someone who isn't a fiduciary could urge the couple to buy one, and then justify the recommendation by claiming that it was somehow "suitable."

Every RIA is required to submit to the Securities and Exchange Commission an ADV form—a document that shows fees, officers, professional history, and possible conflicts. Any RIA with whom you do business is required to provide you with this form. If you are interviewing an RIA, ask to see a copy of this document as part of your due diligence.

Even if you limit your search to investment advisors, you're still not out of the woods. Work exclusively with fee-only advisors: It eliminates a huge conflict of interest. Since these advisors refuse commissions, you won't have to worry about them pushing an investment simply to pocket a sales charge. This leaves the fee-only professionals to work exclusively for you.

Brokers and many financial planners depend on commissions. They keep a lot of clients because their bills are hidden. They never ask you to write a check for their services, which makes customers happy—but these clients don't realize that they're paying dearly through hidden costs.

Fee-only advisors bill clients differently. Many assess their fee based on the value of the client's portfolio. An advisor will often charge an annual 1 percent fee to oversee a client's assets. A client with $500,000 would pay $5,000. Many fee-only professionals will scale back the fee for clients with larger nest eggs, $1 million or higher.

This arrangement isn't going to work for everybody. In fact, it used to be that the fee-only system shut out a lot of middle-class investors who didn't own a big enough portfolio to make a yearly management charge realistic. But today some advisors charge by the hour. Spending a few hundred dollars to consult a competent, ethical, and well-qualified advisor can be well worth the investment.

Look for these advisors through the National Association of Personal Financial Advisors (www.napfa.org), which has roughly one thousand members. Dimensional Fund Advisors (www.dfaus.com) is another resource for fee-only advisors authorized to place clients' assets in its funds. And the Center for Fiduciary Studies (www.fi360 .com/cfstudies) is one of the most passionate institutional advocates of advisors as fiduciaries.

Once you've gathered some names, the trick is finding an advisor with whom you feel comfortable. Often advisors will provide potential customers with a complimentary get-acquainted session. Use those opportunities.

What should you ask during these free sessions? The National Association of Personal Financial Advisors offers a detailed questionnaire to help you interview candidates (The NAPFA Comprehensive Financial Planning Diagnostic).

All advisors should focus on your asset allocation and on the use of low-cost index funds, passively managed funds, or ETFs to implement a portfolio that's consistent with your investment objectives and tolerance for risk.

Any advisor who tells you she can "beat the markets" is about to beat *you* out of your retirement nest egg.

After you find a trustworthy advisor, get her to outline the advisory relationship in writing.

The written agreement should cover the following:

1. The advisor needs to say outright that he or she is a fiduciary—meaning that *your* interests come first.

2. The advisor should inform you of any conflicts of interest—like if he's working for a fund company that he's recommending.

3. The advisor should explain how he is getting paid. It could be a flat fee or a percentage of the value of your assets. He should tell you if he's getting money from any other source, such as a mutual fund.

4. The advisor should explain how he'd provide advice. Legally, his selection of the mutual fund family, the types of mutual funds, or the mix of investments can't affect his compensation.

5. The advisor should agree to determine an appropriate asset allocation for you *and to use low-cost index funds, ETFs, or passively managed funds instead of actively managed funds for your portfolio*. Of all the litmus tests, this is the critical one. You will weed out a lot of candidates before finding one who will agree to handle your assets in this manner. It is worth your time and effort to keep looking until you do.

After talking with you and asking about your investment goals, the advisor should create a participant policy statement (PPS). Then he should meet with you on an annual basis.

Again, most investors don't need any "expert" advice. You can successfully invest by following the basic principles I have laid out here. But for those investors who believe assistance might be helpful, be sure that you don't get stuck with a financial hack who can sabotage your future retirement.

Now you know how to tell the difference.

What's the Point?

- If you feel you need a financial advisor, make sure the advisor is an RIA who will focus on your *asset allocation* and the use of *low-cost index funds* for your portfolio.

CHAPTER 30

It's So Easy, the Government Did It!

The retirement plan Uncle Sam has right. Hard to
believe but true: The government offers employees
a great plan, and you'd do well to emulate it.
—Walter Updegrave, *Money* magazine, November 23, 2006

Jane Bryant Quinn, the respected financial journalist, called it "a perfect 401(k)."

Jim Cramer said the plan offers "one way in which we could cut the costs, keep fees low, offer strict diversification, and make sure that nobody gets ripped off."

It has one of the highest voluntary participation rates in the country—an astounding 86 percent—at a rock-bottom cost of 0.03 percent (three one-hundredths of 1 percent).

It's *huge*. As of July 2007, it had $224 billion in assets, contributed by 3.77 million investors.

What's this plan?

This stellar 401(k) is the Thrift Savings Plan (TSP), created in 1986 after Congress concluded that federal workers should also have a retirement plan.

Unless you're a federal employee—a troop fighting overseas, a

member of Congress, or a Washington, DC, pencil pusher—you probably haven't heard of it.

Its many admirers insist that all employees would be far better off
if 401(k) plans were modeled after this federal program.

Why does the TSP outshine nearly all of the nation's 401(k) plans?

Besides the low cost, the menu holds only a few options—in contrast with the typical 401(k) plan's nineteen choices. Too many choices
tend to bewilder investors, which leads them to make bad decisions.

The TSP's selection also covers all the investment categories that the
typical worker needs to build a diversified portfolio. And each option
under the TSP is a quality, low-cost index fund:

- Government Securities Investment Fund

- Fixed Income Index Investment Fund

- Common Stock Index Investment Fund

- Small Capitalization Stock Index Investment Fund

- International Stock Index Investment Fund

- Lifecycle Funds

The most notable funds on the list are the Lifecycle Funds, also
known as Target Retirement Funds. With these funds, the investor
chooses the date closest to her retirement date. The fund will automatically allocate her assets—domestic stocks, international stocks,
and bonds—and, as she ages, rebalance them *daily* to create a more
conservative portfolio as the target date approaches.

Nothing could be easier: Set it and forget it!

The Thrift Savings Plan seems to prove the old adage about building a better mousetrap. A 2007 survey found that TSP participants are
more satisfied with their retirement plan than their 401(k) peers.

Compare the TSP to your plan. Yours is probably far more costly. It has many more investment options—all the better to confuse you. Most of the choices are probably hyperactively managed mutual funds, with high expense ratios. It's unlikely that you have the option of Target Retirement Funds. If you do, the underlying funds probably aren't low-cost index funds. Most of your fellow employees have no idea how to invest their 401(k) assets, which accounts for their dismal returns.

You deserve a 401(k) that is as good as the Thrift Savings Plan.

You aren't getting one for one basic reason: fees.

No one is feeding at the trough at the Thrift Savings Plan. The fund advisors are not receiving any "revenue sharing" fees that influence their judgment. And government employees are being rewarded for this reality with fatter retirement nest eggs.

There are economies of scale that permit this huge plan to be offered at such a low cost. These economies of scale are not available to smaller plans. However, there is no reason why all 401(k) plans could not follow the basic investment principles represented by this plan and offer similar choices to its participants, even if the costs were higher.

There is no doubt that employees would be immeasurably better off if their 401(k) plans adopted the basic features of the Thrift Savings Plan.

After all, it is good enough for members of Congress!

What's the Point?

- A model 401(k) plan has limited investment options and low expenses.

- It offers low-cost index funds and "set it and forget it" Lifecycle Funds.

CHAPTER 31

Evaluating Your Own 401(k)

**Many 401(k) plans have an endless array of bells and
whistles yet people don't join the plan, don't contribute
enough, or don't invest their money properly.**
—Brooks Hamilton, attorney and employee benefit consultant

I f you've read this far, it's only natural to wonder whether *your* 401(k)
is simply serving as a feeding trough for the financial industry.

Fortunately, this is not difficult.

A good 401(k) plan will give employees one or (preferably) both of
the following options:

1. It will have at least three index funds, ETFs, or passively managed funds from DFA:

- One fund will have as its benchmark the Wilshire 5000, which will
  give employees the broadest exposure to the domestic stock market.

- One fund will have as its benchmark the MSCI AC World Index
  (excluding the United States), which will give employees the
  broadest exposure to a range of international stocks.

- One fund will have as its benchmark the Lehman U.S. Aggregate
  Bond Index, which will give employees the broadest exposure to
  a range of highly rated bonds.

2. It will have as an option a selection of Target Retirement Funds (also called Lifecycle Funds). These funds can be a wonderful solution for anyone who doesn't want to fool with assembling a diversified retirement portfolio. One fund, containing a mix of stocks, bonds, and cash, will accomplish that for you. These funds automatically grow more conservative as you age, which means you may never need to rebalance or look elsewhere.

But be aware of pernicious Lifecycle Funds. Some of these funds are ridiculously expensive and include an extra fee—on top of the underlying investment costs—that can range from .25 percent to 1 percent. Be sure your Lifecycle Fund is one of the many low-cost ones, like the Vanguard Target Retirement Funds.

Also, be sure that the underlying funds are primarily index funds, and not hyperactively managed funds.

If your 401(k) plan has one or both of these options, it passes the smell test and affords you the opportunity to maximize your retirement savings. If it doesn't, you are being penalized.

You should also do the following:

Check the costs of your fund options. Get a copy of each fund's prospectus (a document defining the risk of the investment; you should be able to download these from the fund company's website).

Then look at the expense ratio, which explains what percentage of your assets are automatically sucked out of your account to cover fund costs. Ideally, you want funds that have expense ratios far below 1 percent. This should not be a problem with the index funds, ETFs, and passively managed funds in your plan. It will most likely be a problem with the hyperactively managed funds in your plan.

Find out if you're trapped in an annuity. In a perfect 401(k) world, annuities wouldn't exist. Even aside from the hideous costs, there is no reason why you would need an annuity inside a 401(k). We'll discuss annuities in Part Five, but all you need to know now is that most annuities are *extremely* expensive. It's not unusual to see the yearly expenses for 401(k) annuities ranging from 3 to 5.5 percent.

The costs of annuities are difficult to calculate. Insurers don't have to disclose these expenses to 401(k) investors. However, 401(k) annuity costs must be disclosed in the contract that an employer signs off on. Ask your company for a copy of the contract. If that doesn't work, contact the insurance company. (If you still strike out, complain to your state's insurance commission.)

What's the Point?

- If your 401(k) plan does not give you the option to invest in at least three broad-based, low-cost index funds and a range of Target Retirement Funds, you have a subpar plan.

CHAPTER 32

Lobbying for the 401(k) You Deserve

> Within the 401(k) industry, as assets continue to grow,
> there is a strong argument to be made that we are paying
> more for the servicing of these accounts than needs
> to be paid. Of course, that translates to less money for
> the participants.
>
> —Donald Trone, Center for Fiduciary Studies

Now that you know how the 401(k) industry is gouging you, I hope you're compelled to secure a better plan. Sadly, many employers don't know what's wrong with their 401(k) plans, or why common practices like revenue sharing have jeopardized the financial future of millions of workers.

So to get the best plan possible, *you* need to understand what's happening and what your alternatives are. Here's how:

Request a fee audit. Many company sponsors can't untangle the web of fees—even if they care enough to try. An audit will pinpoint how much money is being generated in the 401(k) and who is pocketing it. An audit can wake your employer up to the magnitude of the fees it's signed off on and will also provide greater bargaining power. Often the current 401(k) provider will be willing to negotiate a lower price rather than risk being given the heave-ho.

Ask your human resources department or plan administrator for a copy of any plan audit. If none has been done recently, suggest that an audit be conducted.

Seek membership on your company's 401(k) investment committee. This is the group that makes decisions about your company's 401(k). At smaller companies, there often is no committee; instead, the bosses will pick a plan. (And they could end up picking a plan based on personal relationships—buying a too-expensive plan from a college fraternity brother or golfing buddy.)

Don't take ignorance as an excuse. Companies that offer 401(k) plans are legally considered to be fiduciaries. As a fiduciary, company executives must understand what all the costs are that are embedded in a 401(k) package. It's only then that they can evaluate whether the services are appropriate and reasonable. If they don't do that, they're violating the Employee Retirement Income Security Act (ERISA), which is the federal law that regulates private pensions and retirement plans.

The "hear no evil, see no evil" attitude of many employers about the fees in their 401(k) plans has triggered class-action lawsuits. The St. Louis law firm of Schlichter, Bogard & Denton filed the first thirteen 401(k) suits in 2006, alleging that employers did nothing about excessive fees that were eroding their workers' accounts. These cases are pending, and there has been no finding of liability or wrongdoing. However, the mere fact that they were filed should be a wake-up call to all employer sponsors of 401(k) plans.

One thing is certain: There is no motivation for employers, 401(k) advisors, and the mutual fund industry to disturb the lucrative and cozy system that is working so well for them.

It is up to *you* to make something positive happen.

What's the Point?

- Lobby for a better 401(k) plan.

- Ask your employer for an audit of the fees in your 401(k) plan.

PART FOUR

The Care and Feeding of Your IRA

CHAPTER 33

The Neglected IRA

I never get tired of talking about the great benefits of IRAs.
—Dan Caplinger, "4 Tips for Your Annual IRA Checkup,"
The Motley Fool, April 5, 2007

We've already discussed IRAs—individual retirement accounts. These are independent accounts that you can hold solo or alongside your 401(k) or other holdings. You can open them directly with low-cost fund families like Vanguard, Fidelity, and T. Rowe Price, or with a broker, like Charles Schwab.

An IRA is *not* an investment. It's not a stock, a mutual fund, an annuity, or a U.S. Treasury bond. An IRA is simply a shell. The account will just sit there until you instruct the financial institution on what to do with the cash you stash in it.

The financial assets of families with IRAs are six times greater than the net worth of households without IRAs. Sadly, fewer than two out of every ten households contribute to an IRA.

Here's why you should be among those that do:

- As discussed earlier, an IRA can be a wonderful substitute if your 401(k) investment lineup looks like roadkill.

- You'll have better investment options. In a 401(k), you're stuck with the mutual funds or (even worse) annuity selected by your employer. With an IRA, you're free to choose your investments.

- An IRA promotes disciplined savings. With an IRA, it's easy to instruct a financial institution to withdraw a certain amount of money—small or large—on a certain date every month from your checking or savings account. Autopilot savings is an excellent way to fatten your nest egg.

- An IRA is a tax cocoon. As long as the cash stays in an IRA, there's no need to worry about taxes. (With a Roth IRA, which we'll discuss in a bit, you won't ever pay taxes.)

- It's the gift that keeps on giving. If you or a loved one inherits an IRA, its value can continue to increase over the years, even as you withdraw money from it.

- An IRA is a tax diversifier. Do you know what's going to happen to income tax rates? Neither do I. If you invest in a Roth IRA, you don't have to worry as much about whether taxes will skyrocket because you won't owe taxes on this money when it's withdrawn.

- An IRA accepts other retirement money. If you're leaving a job and you've got a 401(k), 403(b), or 457(b) plan, you can dump that money into an IRA rollover account.

- An IRA is a welcome tax break. Facing a stiff tax bill in April? Contributing to a traditional IRA will earn you a tax break to shrink what you owe Uncle Sam.

- Some IRAs are dependable lockboxes. If you invest in a Roth IRA, the federal government won't force you to drain it during your retirement. Distributions aren't mandatory.

- An IRA offers generous deadlines. The federal government always gives you a 15½-month cycle to invest in an IRA. For the 2009 tax year, for example, your window of opportunity to contribute extends from January 1, 2009, until April 15, 2010.

Now that you've seen what an IRA can do for you, let's discuss how to open one.

What's the Point?

- Investing in an IRA is a smart option for most investors.

CHAPTER 34

The Nuts and Bolts of IRAs

An IRA is a great way to sock money away for
the future and save on taxes now.
—*The Motley Fool*

If you're among the majority of investors without IRAs, learning their mechanics will help you get in the game. Getting started is easy.

Here's what to do:

1. Open an account. You can establish an IRA at just about any financial institution. (If you want to follow the suggestions in this book and invest in low-cost index funds, find a mutual fund company or discount brokerage firm that offers low-cost index choices.) You can call the firm or visit its website to download the simple IRA forms you'll need.

2. Select a widely diversified fund. If this is your first IRA, you're not going to have a load of cash to spread around. The maximum yearly contribution you can make is $5,000 ($6,000 if you're fifty or older).

If you're just starting out, you might want to select an all-in-one Lifecycle or Target Retirement Fund that spreads your money across a wide swath of investments.

3. **Invest automatically.** If you're like most folks, there will always be more pressing and immediate needs for the money you would invest in an IRA. Fight this natural urge by setting up an automatic monthly savings plan with the financial institution.

4. **Be careful with the handoff.** If you start an IRA by rolling over a 401(k) or 403(b), you will follow many of the same steps as establishing an IRA from scratch. But you will also need to fill out transfer paperwork. This is critical. You absolutely *don't* want your employer to send you a check to your home—it will deduct 20 percent of the account's value for taxes. Getting that money back will be a costly hassle.

But there's another reason why you don't want to touch the money. If the assets aren't deposited into the IRA within sixty days, the IRA will implode and you'll owe taxes on all that cash.

5. **Use free advice.** Not everybody needs or wants to hire a financial professional. But you may be entitled to free or inexpensive advice if you move your cash to certain discount brokerage firms and fund companies such as Vanguard, T. Rowe Price, Fidelity Investments, and Charles Schwab. Beyond assisting you with the mechanics of starting or moving an IRA, advisors can help you with common questions regarding savings goals, asset allocation, and tapping into a nest egg during retirement. If you have enough money with the firm, you'll pay little or nothing for the advice.

Many of you will need little or no assistance. All these firms have crammed their websites full of nifty online financial tools.

What's the Point?

- Opening an IRA is quick and easy.

CHAPTER 35

Fall in Love with the Roth IRA

If you're confused about which type of retirement account to choose, here's the quick and easy (and probably smartest) strategy: Put your money in a Roth IRA.

—Robert Brokamp, *The Motley Fool*

So I've sold you on IRAs—but which one should you choose? A Roth IRA or a deductible (traditional) IRA?

First, you have to determine whether you earn too much income to qualify for a Roth. If you are a single filer and have a modified adjusted gross income of more than $101,000, you are not eligible to make a full contribution to a Roth IRA. For joint filers, that number increases to $159,000. You may still be able to make a partial contribution if you are a single filer and your modified adjusted gross income is between $101,000 and $116,000, or a joint filer with a Modified Adjusted Gross Income of $159,000–$169,000.

Assuming that a Roth IRA is an option, here's a rundown of the Roth IRA and the traditional IRA:

They're both tax-deferred accounts. But unlike a traditional IRA, Roth IRA contributions are made with already-taxed income. This is usually the preferable option, as you'll soon see.

The deductible, or traditional, IRA's biggest selling point is its promise of instant gratification. You earn a tax deduction (determined by your income tax bracket) for all your IRA contributions. If you invest $3,000 in a deductible IRA and you're in the 15 percent tax bracket, for instance, you'd get to reduce your federal tax bill by $450. The amount of your deduction will be lessened once your modified adjusted gross income reaches a certain level.

That might sound great, but the IRS will eventually gobble up your account like a cheap Las Vegas buffet. When you retire and start draining the account, you'll owe income tax on all your withdrawals. And you can only put off these withdrawals for so long. Even if you don't need the money, the IRS forces you to make yearly withdrawals shortly after reaching the age of 70½.

Those mandatory withdrawals could end up boosting your income tax bracket (and we cannot predict what ordinary income tax rates will be in the future). The extra income could also trigger taxes on your Social Security checks . . . a perfect storm of taxes.

In contrast, the Roth IRA doesn't offer a tax deduction for contributions (you are contributing with after-tax dollars), but there's also no penalty for early withdrawals. You won't pay taxes on withdrawals up to the amount contributed, and there's no tax on investment earnings within the Roth IRA once you reach age 59½ (or become disabled), provided that the account was in existence for five or more years.

So Roth investors who tap into a Roth after they retire won't pay *any* taxes on their withdrawals. That could save you tens—if not hundreds—of thousands of dollars.

What's more, the government won't force you to take any money out while you're alive, so you can leave the Roth to your heirs—who still won't have to pay income taxes when they withdraw whatever's left.

The choice is simple: If you don't need the tax break immediately, go with the Roth IRA. The immediate tax deductions of the traditional IRA are more than offset by the overall benefits of the Roth IRA.

What's the Point?

- A Roth IRA offers more benefits than a traditional IRA.

CHAPTER 36

Want to Leave Your IRA to the USA?

**A taxpaying public that doesn't understand the law is a
taxpaying public that can't comply with the law.**
—Lawrence Gibbs, commissioner, Internal Revenue Service

It's morbid to consider, but necessary: What's going to happen to your IRA after you die?

You have to ask yourself this question because you can't trust someone else—your financial advisor, for instance—to ask (and answer) it for you.

A broker who has your IRA account probably isn't going to check to see whether the beneficiary forms on the account remain current. So if his client dies and his client's ex-wife inherits his IRA—because nobody told the former husband to update the form by naming his kids or a second wife as beneficiaries—well, that's the way it goes. The ex-wife, who will legally collect the windfall, will be incredibly grateful for your sloppiness.

Here's what you should do if you want to bequeath your IRA the right way:

- **Name a person—not your "estate"—as a beneficiary.** You'd be surprised how many people name their estate as the beneficiary.

When that happens, your heirs are drop-kicked into the world of probate. Probate is the often tedious, cumbersome, and expensive legal procedure for settling the affairs of an individual who has died and transferring his or her property to the rightful beneficiaries.

What's worse, an IRA left to an estate shortens the tax deferral life of the IRA. If you die before age 70½, the entire IRA must be distributed (and taxed) by the end of the fifth year after your death.

If you die after the age of 70½, the length of the required payout will be determined by your life expectancy. While this may (or may not) be more than five years, it will often be far less than the payout permitted if the IRA was left to an individual and not to your estate.

If you name your spouse as the beneficiary of your IRA, they get to treat the inherited IRA just like it was their own—a major benefit.

If you name a nonspouse as the beneficiary of your IRA, they have the option to have the inherited IRA paid out over *their* life expectancy. Of course, unless it is a Roth IRA, the beneficiary has to pay ordinary income taxes on the amount he or she receives each year. This option must be selected no later than December 31 of the year following your death.

This can be a major benefit. For example, naming your grandchild as the beneficiary of your IRA could extend the tax-deferral life of the IRA by decades.

- **Keep copies of IRA forms.** Don't assume that the bank or brokerage house is keeping your beneficiary forms. With so many financial institutions merging over the years, your papers could get lost in a warehouse three thousand miles away.

- **Appoint a secondary beneficiary.** You aren't out of the woods just because you leave your IRA to your spouse. What happens if your spouse dies before you do, or you're both killed in the same accident?

You can preserve the tax benefits of an IRA by appointing a "contingent beneficiary" (a person who will inherit your IRA in the event that your primary beneficiary dies before you do). Otherwise, it's possible that the death of the primary beneficiary may cause the IRA to be deemed left to his or her estate, with all of the adverse tax consequences that that entails.

What's the Point?

- Never leave an IRA to your estate.

- Be sure the beneficiary forms for your IRA are updated and in order.

- Appoint a primary *and* a contingent beneficiary.

PART FIVE

403(b) Plans and Annuities—They Make 401(k) Plans Look Good!

CHAPTER 37

403(b) Plans:
A National Disgrace

These plans are typically offered to public school teachers, among others. I approach them with a heavy heart.
—Jane Bryant Quinn, "Smart and Simple Financial Strategies for Busy People"

I f you work in a public school, a hospital, or a not-for-profit, or are a member of the clergy, you should feel like a valued member of your community.

But you wouldn't know it from the way your retirement plan operates.

Your plan, named for the 403(b) section in the Internal Revenue Code, *looks* legitimate enough. Participants make pretax contributions, and employers will match them, as in 401(k) plans. As long as the cash stays in the 403(b) cocoon, the employee won't have to worry about getting dinged with taxes.

A diligent saver pockets a tax deduction for the cash he squirrels away into one of these accounts. So if a teacher is in the 25 percent tax bracket and invests $5,000 for the year, he'll get a $1,250 reduction in his tax liability.

But like 401(k) plans, when you retire and begin tapping into your 403(b) account, you'll owe ordinary income taxes on all withdrawals.

Unfortunately, employers are even less involved with 403(b) plans than they are with 401(k) plans.

With 401(k) plans, the employer at least sets up and administers a plan, giving employees a lineup of funds to choose from. Kind of like a menu at a Chinese restaurant, except typically with worse choices.

But Congress must have thought that even this modest level of involvement was too much to ask of school districts. They don't have to set up or administer a plan. They don't even have an obligation to run the plan in the best interests of their employees.

They give no advice or guidance. They only match the contributions from the salaries of their (underpaid) employees and designate the financial institutions where the employees are permitted to invest—usually doing them a major disservice in the process.

These plans offer worse investment options than the high-expense-ratio, underperforming, hyperactively managed funds that populate most 401(k) plans.

Congress singled out some of the most worthy members of our society and basically made them cannon fodder for the insurance and securities industries.

When 403(b) plans were first created in 1958, participants were permitted to invest only in annuities. This must have been considered a brilliant accomplishment by the insurance lobby.

Annuities are tax-deferred contracts that combine the worst elements of an investment portfolio with an overpriced "death benefit." Typically, they're high-cost, high-commission, and high-penalty investment vehicles that are suitable for precious few investors, even outside of a retirement plan. And they're particularly bad investments within a plan, where the tax deferral they offer is like wearing a raincoat indoors.

Mercifully, the law was changed in 1974, and now many 403(b) plans allow investments in mutual funds (although some school districts inexplicably approve only annuity providers).

This unique set of regulatory lapses created both chaos and a perfect storm for abuse.

No advice or guidance. The lure of easy prey of unsophisticated investors. A bias toward an investment that's inappropriate but lucrative for its salespeople. And a huge market: Some estimates place 403(b) contributions at around $700 billion.

And since investments in 403(b) plans are sold directly to individual employees, school lounges around the country host a daily feeding frenzy, as annuity salesmen descend upon teachers like vultures, pitching their retirement products. Teachers sign up in droves, believing that they're making an intelligent choice and providing for their retirement needs.

Little do they know that most of them have made a terrible decision that violates all of the Smart Investing principles in this book—and then some.

They deserve much better.

What's the Point?

- 403(b) plans are a trap for the unwary.

- Annuities are rarely good investment options.

CHAPTER 38

Looking for Help in All the Wrong Places

403(b) retirement plans reside in the "dankest, foulest-smelling cellars of the financial world."

—William Bernstein, *The Four Pillars of Investing*

In the absence of any advice from school districts, many teachers look to their unions for investment guidance. Often they're asking the fox to protect the chickens: Many of these unions are steering their members to junkyard 403(b) plans.

Why? Because they're getting kickbacks from the insurance companies and financial firms they endorse. Sometimes the kickbacks are direct payments. Other times the investment providers advertise in union publications or sponsor union conferences.

Sound familiar? This conduct bears an eerie resemblance to the "revenue sharing" payments that brokers and advisors extract for placing favored mutual funds in 401(k) plans.

Some of the cash windfalls received by these unions are stunningly high. The *Los Angeles Times* revealed that the New York State United Teachers union was receiving $3 million a year from ING Group, a major insurance player.

The National Education Association (NEA) hauled in close to

$50 million in royalties in just *one* year from the sale of annuities, insurance, and other products it endorsed.

But teachers have started fighting back. After the *Los Angeles Times* story, teachers sued the NEA for allegedly breaching its duty.

How did these cozy arrangements start? Traditionally, school districts haven't investigated their employees' 403(b) providers. So it's been easy for 403(b) vendors—primarily insurance companies—to be approved by a district, meaning that some districts had dozens of providers peddling their products. That's even more confusing than sifting through the limited choices in a 401(k) plan!

And school districts have done little or nothing to monitor the performance of the investments sold to their employees or to ask about fees. This hands-off stance created a welcome opening for commission-hungry stockbrokers and insurance agents.

As you'll learn later, schools, hospitals, and charities are now being forced to change their ways.

What's the Point?

- Don't assume your union or administrator has your best interests at heart when it endorses 403(b) investment options.

CHAPTER 39

The Annuity Scam

In the process of delivering investment products to public
school teachers (and employees of non-profits) enrolled
in 403(b) plans, the main focus is on the convenience and
(unreasonable) profitability of the insurance companies
that distribute such products. Little more than lip service is
paid to what's best for the welfare of plan participants.
—W. Scott Simon, *Morningstar Advisor*, May 3, 2007

Annuities sold to unwitting participants in 403(b) plans (and outside of them as well) come in three flavors:

1. A variable annuity;

2. A fixed annuity; and

3. An equity indexed annuity, which is a variant of a fixed annuity.

All annuities share one common purpose: to provide a series of payments over a period of time.

With a variable annuity, the purchaser of the annuity chooses the investment options, typically from high-expense, hyperactively managed funds offered by insurance companies. Often these funds are "house funds," managed by the insurance company. If the funds are managed by outside fund families, the expenses are inflated to help the fund sponsors make the required payments to the insurance company for this "shelf space."

With a fixed annuity, the insurance company takes responsibility for making the investments and, in exchange, guarantees a "fixed" interest rate to the holder of the annuity.

With an equity indexed annuity, the purchaser is promised an investment vehicle that earns interest typically linked to a benchmark index, like the S&P 500. These contracts usually provide for a minimum guaranteed rate of interest and also place a floor below which the value of the annuity will not fall, regardless of the performance of the benchmark.

A major selling point for all kinds of annuities is the fact that the appreciation in the annuity is sheltered from taxes until it is withdrawn.

"Tax deferral" seems great, right?

But all investments in a 403(b) plan are *already* tax deferred, so there's no additional tax benefit to placing an annuity within the plan. Indeed, buying an annuity within a 403(b) plan for its "tax deferral benefits" is no different than buying a cup of air at McDonald's.

But here's the kicker when it comes to all types of annuities—a very simple reason why they're such a bad idea: The costs of 403(b) annuities can range from 2 to 5 percent—putting these investments squarely in bloodsucking territory. These fees can be as much as *800 percent higher* than the fees charged by mutual funds.

800 percent higher!

Thankfully, there's a notable exception to high-cost annuity providers: TIAA-CREF (with whom I have no affiliation). Think of it as the "Vanguard" of annuity providers. TIAA-CREF's fixed and variable annuities are among the lowest cost anywhere. And unlike most of its competitors, its annuities have no surrender charges. Surrender charges penalize early withdrawals—another reason why most annuities are a bad choice.

Many teachers aren't aware of the TIAA-CREF option because TIAA-CREF doesn't hire commission salesmen to hustle business in school lounges.

As I noted earlier, 403(b) participants no longer have to be stuck with annuities in their plan. Many 403(b) plans offer mutual funds. Nevertheless, close to 80 percent of teachers are still investing in annuities.

For some teachers it's because they aren't given a choice: Annuities are all they're offered. Others simply are not aware of their options.

Members of the clergy also have options. Churches and related organizations can set up retirement income accounts. These accounts may invest in annuities and mutual funds. Participants in these accounts would also be well advised to avoid annuities and invest in low-cost index funds.

Here's the bottom line: The vast majority of those 403(b) participants with annuities would be better off in low-cost mutual funds. We'll explore this in more detail in the next chapter.

What's the Point?

- If your only option is an annuity, choose low-cost annuities offered by TIAA-CREF.

- If you have the option, invest in low-cost index funds, following the investing principles in this book.

CHAPTER 40

Feeding at the
Annuity Trough

**It's a rare school district that gives teachers access to quality
choice. In most cases, they just turn a blind eye to the problems.**
—Dan Otter, former teacher and founder of 403bwise.com, an
advocacy site for 403(b) investors

t's rarely obvious just how much annuities gouge their owners until
years later, when retirees wonder why their nest egg looks like a
canary's instead of an ostrich's.

Here's an example:

Suppose a young teacher decided to invest $100 a month into an
annuity that generated an annual return of 8.5 percent. The fees for
this expensive plan totaled 4 percent. (Yes, fees can balloon this high.)
After forty years, the teacher's account would be worth $134,618. If he
had socked away $200 a month, the account would ultimately reach
$269,236.

That seems respectable—but look at the difference if our young
teacher had invested in low-cost mutual funds rather than a high-cost
annuity. If the same teacher had invested $100 a month in these low-
cost funds, charging only 0.5 in expenses, after forty years he'd have
$351,428, assuming he earned the same 8.5 percent returns. And if the

teacher had invested $200 a month, the account would have mushroomed to an amazing $702,856.

I don't know about you, but I doubt that many people can afford to turn their backs on an extra $216,810, much less $433,620.

Expenses *really* matter.

The typical annuity imposes fees that far exceed those you would find in low-cost index funds. The lineup of total fees follows. Some of these fees are also incurred by mutual funds, but it is the totality of these fees that is a source of concern.

Investment management fees. Charged just for investing the money in an account. Look for investments that carry the lowest possible charge.

Brokerage commissions and trading costs. Charged to cover the cost of trading. Sometimes these costs can be influenced by "soft dollar" arrangements, in which the brokerage firm provides research to the funds in exchange for the fund using the broker to execute trades. This can result in higher brokerage commissions.

Mortality and expense fees. This is one of the biggest rip-offs. This fee dings you for the annuity's insurance. It's a pointless extra cost, since the insurance typically only kicks in if your annuity's ending balance, upon your death, is lower than the sum of all your contributions over the years—a very rare occurrence. If the balance is lower, your heirs will receive the equivalent of all your contributions, minus any withdrawals you made.

Custodial fee. Charged just for holding the securities in the account. (As if you weren't paying enough already!)

Transfer fee. Charged if you move money either to another fund that's offered within the same company or to an outside company.

Surrender charges. Charged to clients who leave too soon. These charges can last ten years or even longer.

Surrender charges are a particularly nasty fee. Here's why: Salespeople make incredible commissions from these plans. But the insurance companies don't want to pay their sales force only to see their customers wander off the reservation before the sales commissions are recouped . . . many times over.

Surrender charges usually shrink a percentage point every year. So if your annuity has a 7 percent surrender charge, you'd have to pay 7 percent of your account the first year of the contract if you bailed. The next year the surrender charge would drop to 6 percent.

What's even worse? "Rolling" surrender charges, in which the time period is reset with each new contribution.

Add all of these fees together and what do you get?

An investment that is unsuitable for virtually all participants in 403(b) plans!

What's the Point?

- The high cost and hidden fees of annuities make them a terrible choice for most 403(b) participants.

CHAPTER 41

Variable Annuity Rip-Off

If the terms [of variable annuities] are so terrible, then why do people
buy the salesman's pitch? Because they are mesmerized by the words
"tax deferral." Does this sound familiar? A generation ago a different
crop of investors was mesmerized by the words "tax shelter"—and
ended up with worthless railcar leases and cattle farms.
—Carolyn T. Geer, *Forbes* magazine, February 9, 1998

Variable annuities are poor investments for 403(b) participants
and for most investors who purchase them outside of a retirement plan.

But before you can understand why, you need to know what makes
them tick.

The variable annuity is an insurance product combined with an
investment portfolio, including pooled investment accounts managed by recognizable companies such as Fidelity Investments, T. Rowe
Price, and American Funds. The investment portfolio itself behaves
just like a mutual fund, although in insurance lingo it is called a
"sub-account."

Because these deferred annuities are intended for retirement, you'll
be penalized for pulling your money out before reaching the age of 59½.

Just like a traditional individual retirement account, these annuities act as tax cocoons. Taxes aren't triggered until the owner pulls

out the cash. Unlike an IRA, however, you can stuff as much money as you'd like inside a variable annuity that is outside of a retirement plan. (Salesmen will probably tell you "the more cash, the better," since they'll earn higher commissions.)

Variable annuities also permit a more relaxed withdrawal schedule. An IRA owner, shortly after reaching the age of 70½, must begin pulling money out of his account based on a federal life expectancy chart. Most of the time, you don't have to start draining a variable annuity until you reach the age of eighty-five.

So what's so bad about them?

Let's take a look at the annuity's promises one by one:

The much-hyped "death benefit" draws in customers who are fearful of the stock market's periodic hissy fits. No need to worry, the salesman will insist: If you invest in a deferred variable annuity, the insurer will guarantee that after you die, your heirs will receive the total of all the contributions, minus any withdrawals.

So if you sank $100,000 into the annuity and you die when your account balance has dropped to $80,000 because of the market, your loved ones will still pocket the $100,000.

This might sound great, but let's take a closer look. This guarantee won't benefit the paying customer. If the market declined during your lifetime and your account lost $20,000 of its original $100,000 value, *you* don't get it back. You'd have to die first. The insurance company only kicks in the benefit at the time of your death if your account is less than the original amount invested.

And it's not likely that the benefit will kick in, anyway. What are the odds that an annuity you purchased for $100,000 will be worth *less* than $100,000 fifteen or twenty years later? In order for the death benefit to have any meaningful value, the investor would have to be in poor health and the assets in the sub-accounts would have to be losing a meaningful portion of their original value. That's not a very likely set of circumstances.

Okay, so it's not much of a benefit. So what's the harm? Again, it's cost. This insurance is so expensive that it might as well be encased in gold. Annuities typically charge a fee of 1.25 percent for the life insurance portion, but according to a Goldman Sachs/York University study, the fee should be closer to a mere 0.15 percent! That's more than 800 percent *more* expensive than it should be.

Annuity salesmen also rave about the fact that the appreciation in the investment accounts of an annuity is tax deferred. But you now know that tax deferral in a 403(b) plan is of zero value because the appreciation on all investments in these plans is *already* tax deferred. Therefore, an annuity is particularly unsuitable when it is part of a tax-deferred plan.

Finally, when you withdraw money from one of these annuities, you'll be taxed on the increase in value of the annuity at the ordinary income tax rate that's applicable to you at that time, losing the historically far more favorable rates that govern long-term capital gains (currently 15 percent) and qualified dividend income. If you'd simply invested in low-cost index funds, outside of an annuity, you'd get the benefit of these lower rates—at a much lower cost.

What's the Point?

- Variable annuities rarely make sense for investors in 403(b) plans or outside of them.

CHAPTER 42

Equity Indexed Annuities Are Inequitable

The net result of equity-indexed annuities' complex
formulas and hidden costs is that they survive as the most
confiscatory investments sold to retail investors.
—Craig McCann, PhD, and Dengpan Luo, PhD, "An Overview of
Equity-Indexed Annuities"

Equity indexed annuities (EIAs) are the new flavor of the month for annuity salesmen pitching their 403(b) wares to unsuspecting teachers. They're also aggressively sold to investors outside of retirement plans.

The reality?

They're not suitable for *anyone*.

These are complex insurance products that promise to provide the investor with a return that tracks the stock market's performance. Some salesmen brag that an EIA will earn 100 percent of the performance of the Standard & Poor's 500 index.

Even better, they insist—the customer faces no risk. Even if the stock market craters, the annuity guarantees them a minimum return over the life of the contract. You'll *always* get at least that minimum return.

No risk, and a great reward. At least that's the spiel. Maybe that's why approximately $25 billion in EIAs are sold every year.

But the "no risk–great reward" doesn't pencil out—it never does! In fact, it's not even close, because the calculations used to determine how much money an investor will ultimately pocket from an EIA are rigged against them.

Insurance agents and other annuity peddlers promote these annuities as miracle investments that deliver great stock market returns while protecting their owners from Wall Street's occasional crash-and-burn routines. But that's simply not true. Equity indexed annuities have as much chance of making investors rich as a handful of Monopoly money.

Despite what salesmen say, the annuity's upside potential is significantly limited. You might be told you'll earn 70 percent, or even 100 percent, of the S&P 500 or some other index. That percentage is hogwash because it isn't linked to the benchmark's entire gain.

Insurers, for starters, don't consider the market's dividends when calculating returns. Annuities also impose caps on market gains, and the guaranteed rate of return is typically not applied to 100 percent of the amount invested.

There are probably 100 different ways for insurance companies to determine an EIA's value. No matter what, investors will typically be stuck with a prickly product that is likely to generate lower returns than a simple portfolio of low-risk bonds and a broadly diversified stock index fund.

The penalties can be fierce for anybody who tries to pull their money out prematurely. Surrender charges are often 10 to 12 percent of the investment and sometimes as high as 25 percent.

Many EIAs are sold to elderly investors who don't realize that they have to keep the bulk of their money in the annuity for ten years or more to keep from triggering onerous charges.

So why are they so popular?

Supersized commissions are a big reason. If you knew you'd be pocketing a 10 or 12 percent commission for selling an EIA—far more than commissions from mutual funds—you'd probably have a hard time holding back from pushing one on an unsuspecting customer, too.

State and federal regulators have been investigating EIA sales practices. Florida prosecutors, for example, have filed cases against salesmen who have sold these annuities to senior citizens suffering from dementia. Trial attorneys have initiated numerous lawsuits alleging deceptive sales practices.

Luckily, there are plenty of options for people who are leery about potential stock market volatility.

If you can't afford to lose any cash, stick with a money market and/or an FDIC-insured certificate of deposit.

You could also significantly reduce your risk by pulling together a portfolio that invests 80 percent in a short-term bond index fund and the rest in a stock index fund. Remember the discussion about asset allocation in Chapter 13? If you have the right asset allocation, you will not be concerned about short-term market volatility.

Plenty of people are tempted to invest in these annuities after hearing about them on radio infomercials and during seminars that offer free food. But they're terrible investments for investors outside of a retirement plan, and *worse* within a plan.

Just walk away from the folks peddling them.

What's the Point?

- Equity indexed annuities are great for salesmen—and terrible investments for just about everybody else.

CHAPTER 43

Divorcing an Annuity

In general, these annuities are not a good product for older citizens.
—William Galvin, Secretary of the Commonwealth of Massachusetts

Many investors have dumped hundreds of thousands of dollars or more into dubious annuities because they get hooked by smooth sales pitches.

Insurance agents and commissioned salesmen hypnotize unwary investors into buying variable annuities, as well as the hot equity indexed annuities, by repeating this mantra: *Annuities are safe. Your money is safe. We guarantee that you can't lose money.*

It all sounds great—until long after the contracts are filed away and investors begin to realize they've been snookered.

In Chapters 41 and 42, you learned why deferred variable annuities and equity indexed annuities are poor choices. A well-diversified portfolio of low-cost index funds will almost always trump the returns of a variable or equity indexed annuity.

But what if you already own annuities? Here are some ways to do damage control:

1. Withdraw what you can. Find out if you can withdraw any cash that isn't charged the surrender fee. (This will be the amount that's been invested long enough to have passed the fee mark.) If you can, get this money out of your high-cost annuity and invest in low-cost index funds (but be sure you understand the tax consequences of any withdrawal).

For those funds that are subject to a surrender charge, you will have to assess how you might fare if you bit the bullet, paid the charge, and made the switch to a low-cost annuity or to low-cost index funds.

2. Educate yourself. My book *Does Your Broker Owe You Money?* (Perigee Books, 2006) will give you a good idea of whether or not you may have a claim against your broker.

3. Speak up. Contact the brokerage firm that sold you the annuity or convinced you to switch from one annuity into another. Explain that you're willing to file a complaint with the Financial Industry Regulatory Authority, the securities industry regulator, and the state insurance commission. You may be able to negotiate a resolution.

4. Hire a lawyer. You may want to consult with a securities arbitration attorney who specializes in recovering losses caused by broker misconduct. You can find a lawyer in your geographic area by going to the website of the Public Investors Arbitration Bar Association, www.piaba.org.

5. Switch now or wait? When people discover that their high-cost annuities have fangs, they often sit tight rather than trigger nasty surrender charges. This is often a mistake.

For example, let's assume your variable annuity has a total cost of 2.39 percent (the industry average). If you exchange to a Vanguard annuity with an average cost of .57 percent a year, and add a 1.00 percent surrender fee, your total annual cost with Vanguard would be 1.57 percent—an immediate savings of .82 percent a year (2.39 percent – 1.57 percent). At the end of the old annuity surrender fee, your annual cost would decrease again to .57 percent a year from the original 2.39 percent. We are talking "averages." Many annuities have much higher costs, and your savings could be that much greater.

If the calculations seem too complicated, look for an hourly fee-only planner who should be able to easily crunch the numbers, or ask your accountant to run them for you.

6. **Consider a 1035 exchange.** If your annuity is in a nonqualified account, you can use a 1035 exchange (a provision in the tax code that allows for the transfer of funds from one annuity policy to another without creating a taxable event) to move the money into a cheaper annuity without triggering taxes. The transfer, however, won't shield you from surrender charges. Be wary of brokers and insurance agents who suggest you switch to another annuity; they may only be interested in collecting a commission. A 1035 exchange isn't necessary if your annuity is inside a retirement account, since it already provides tax protection against transfers among any investments. Consider low-cost annuity providers such as TIAA-CREF, Vanguard, Fidelity Investments, and Charles Schwab.

7. **Understand equity indexed annuity challenges.** It's much tougher liberating your cash from an EIA. While many variable annuities are sold through brokerage firms, insurance agents are the prime peddlers of EIAs. It's typically a lot harder for victimized investors to get relief from an insurance carrier or even a state insurance department, which are often far more interested in protecting the powerful insurance industry than their victims.

8. **Use the back door.** If the surrender charges are too onerous to allow you to bail, use the free withdrawal privileges. EIAs, as well as variable annuities, typically allow an investor to withdraw 10 percent of the annuity's value each year without triggering a surrender charge.

Make sure you rescue the greatest amount allowed through this back door, but be sure to determine the tax consequences of these withdrawals before pulling the trigger.

Of course, the best advice is to avoid becoming an "annuity victim" in the first place. Just say *no*!

What's the Point?

- Explore available options for escaping your high-cost annuity.

- Consider retaining a lawyer to see if you have a claim against your broker or insurance salesman.

CHAPTER 44

Standing Up to Goliath— and Winning!

School district officials have enormous purchasing power that
can be used to the full advantage of their participants; they
shouldn't think for a minute that the providers can push them
around and make them conform to their silly requirements.

—W. Scott Simon, *Morningstar Advisor*, August 2, 2007

Think you can't fight back against your school district's horrible
403(b) plan? New Jersey math teacher Bruce McNutt did. A few
years ago, he ran the numbers to determine how much he was
paying for the options available to him in his 403(b) plan. What he
found appalled him.

The three annuity providers in his district's lineup were charging
as much as 3 percent a year. He realized that he'd be much better off
investing in Vanguard's 403(b) plan, which offers mutual funds that
cost far, far less.

But the district blocked its teachers from investing in Vanguard.

McNutt wasn't deterred. He organized seminars for his fellow
teachers, explaining how they were being fleeced. After about one
hundred teachers became equally angry, the district gave in and
added Vanguard to its list of 403(b) providers.

Yes, the employee *can* win.

If you want to lobby for a better 403(b), enlist support from coworkers. Ask your employer to offer low-cost mutual funds from firms like Vanguard, T. Rowe Price, and Fidelity. These firms offer low-cost funds in part because they don't pay salesmen to find customers. You have to contact them directly, but the effort is definitely worth it.

If annuities are offered in the plan, they should be low-fee annuities, with no-load mutual funds (mutual funds sold directly to the investor) and no surrender charges, like those offered by TIAA-CREF.

In lobbying for a better plan, write a letter to all the decision makers. In school districts, that would include the superintendent, the school board members, and the head of human resources.

I have included a sample letter in Appendix C. Send it on your own or, better yet, collect signatures from your colleagues.

What's the Point?

- It is possible to lobby for a better 403(b) plan from your employer.

CHAPTER 45

Taking on the Sacred Cow

When we look at TIAA-CREF, the manager that controls
over half of all 403(b) assets and serves nearly half of the
6.8 million 403(b) participants, we find that over a recent
8.75-year period, the menu of choices available from
TIAA-CREF substantially underperformed what could have been
achieved by the addition of a small number of index funds.

—John Angus, William O. Brown, Janet Kiholm Smith, and
Richard L. Smith, "What's in Your 403(b)? Academic Retirement
Plans and the Costs of Underdiversification," April 18, 2006

TIAA-CREF, the investment management firm, has a lock on the
403(b) plan market in the majority of colleges and universities.
Almost all of these institutions offer funds managed by TIAA-
CREF, and some even limit the options available to plan participants
to those managed by this firm.

TIAA-CREF manages more than $400 billion of assets. A good chunk
of this money is from 403(b) plan participants. The variable annuities
managed by TIAA-CREF have low fees and no surrender charges. So, is
it a good idea for 403(b) participants to invest solely in these annuities?

One study found that 403(b) plan participants who had the option
of investing in both index funds *and* TIAA-CREF annuities could *double* their retirement fund assets.

TIAA-CREF also offers a menu of mutual funds, including index funds.

The study found that restricting participants to investments in the mutual funds available to participants at that time from TIAA-CREF, rather than permitting them to invest in a selection of low-cost index funds from Vanguard or others, also caused a meaningful diminution in their returns.

The study reached this startling conclusion: "To put these figures on a macroeconomic scale, if all TIAA-CREF participants were restricted to only TIAA-CREF over a forty-year horizon, our estimate of the terminal wealth loss is between $700 billion and $4.2 trillion, depending on the mix of investor sophistication levels."

Here's the bottom line:

While TIAA-CREFF does have annuities with lower costs than most, you would still be well advised to avoid annuities and invest in low-cost index funds or in Target Retirement Funds that consist of low-cost index funds.

What's the Point?

- 403(b) participants should have the option of investing both in low-cost index funds and in Target Retirement Funds consisting of low-cost index funds.

CHAPTER 46

Help Is on the Way

New 403(b) regulations which will go into effect January 1, 2009,
offer employers a unique opportunity to drastically improve
the quality and cost of their 403(b) retirement plan.
—"The Employer Get Wise Guide to the New 403(b) Regs," 403bwise.com

Now is a great time to be making noise about 403(b) plans, because the system is about to undergo a revolutionary change. The federal Department of Labor's new 403(b) regulations, which will take effect January 1, 2009, will force employers to take greater responsibility for these retirement plans.

Assuming your employer will immediately become a more conscientious caretaker is probably foolhardy, so it makes sense to understand what changes are afoot.

The new regulations will force employers to pay attention and start analyzing every investment provider that wants to do business with its employees. In this way, they won't be able to just blindly sign off if yet another insurance agent pushes an annuity on an unsuspecting teacher.

Employers will also be forced to develop an investment policy statement, to create guidelines that they must follow when picking and monitoring investment options. An investment policy committee will also have to meet regularly to evaluate the performance and expenses of the investment menu, as well as any employee education.

Federal regulators hope that mandating this review will ultimately lead to wiser choices—namely, once a conscientious investment policy committee discovers that an annuity is charging outrageous fees, it won't want to keep it.

And for the first time, employers must create a written plan document containing eligibility requirements, contribution limits, loan availability, transfer and rollover policies, as well as details on all the 403(b) providers and their investment choices. Employees will have access to this document.

Industry observers believe that the comprehensive new rules will encourage employers to dramatically reduce the number of 403(b) providers and to ensure that the ones selected offer appropriate investment options, at reasonable costs, to participants in the plan.

In the end, the buck stops with you. Don't let your employer leave you with a smaller nest egg than you deserve. *You* need to take control of your own finances—and you can.

What's the Point?

- New regulations should improve your 403(b) plan, but you need to remain vigilant.

CHAPTER 47

Does a Better Past Mean a Better Future?

Thanks to recent tax law changes the 457(b) is now a viable investment option for many educators. School districts across the country are beginning to offer this plan to their employees and you should be aware of the many benefits it has to offer.

—Scott Dauenhauer, "The 457(b) for Teachers: A Planner's Take"

Teachers and other governmental employees have another arrow in their retirement quiver: a 457(b) plan.

This plan is very similar to the 403(b) plan. It permits teachers and other governmental employees to make pretax contributions to the plan. There is the same tax-deferral benefit under this plan as is available under a 403(b) plan.

The employer deducts the amount of the contribution (up to a maximum of $15,500 per year, although there are a number of exceptions) and invests it with a designated investment entity.

Eligible employees can contribute to both 403(b) and 457(b) plans, subject to the maximum contribution (currently $31,000).

What is the major difference between 403(b) plans and 457(b) plans?

In a 457(b) plan, there's no penalty for an early withdrawal (prior to age 59½) of assets in the plan.

At the end of the day, the plans' investment options should be the key issue when deciding whether to invest in a 457(b), a 403(b), or both.

Another benefit of 457(b) plans is that they don't have the same unfortunate history as 403(b) plans. Unlike 403(b) plans, 457(b) participants were never relegated to annuities. As a consequence, 457(b) plans include mutual funds as the dominant option.

Smart Investors may have more of an ability to implement their asset allocation with an appropriate selection of low-cost index funds in 457(b) plans rather than in 403(b) plans. If so, this fact should influence your decision.

If your 457(b) plan offers an array of low-cost Target Retirement Funds, all the better.

What's the Point?

- Consider investing in a 457(b) plan in addition to your other plan options.

PART SIX

Alternatives to Traditional Retirement Plans

Deferred Compensation Plans for Highly Compensated Employees: A Good Deal . . . for the Securities Industry!

It's amazing what contortions people will endure to avoid paying a small tax.
—Ashlea Ebeling, "Deferral Games," *Forbes* magazine, February 9, 2007

There are some alternatives to the more traditional retirement plans that may be worthy of consideration.

Some large companies offer their most highly compensated employees a plan known as a deferred compensation plan. This plan allows the employee to defer more income than their 401(k) plans permit.

Here's how they typically work.

- Designated employees can defer a large chunk of their income—typically up to 70 percent of their salary.

- The tax on the amount deferred and any appreciation on that money is deferred until it is withdrawn.

- There is no penalty for an early withdrawal under most circumstances.

What a deal! Right?

Wrong.

As we saw with most 401(k) plans, your investments are limited to those in the plan. Typically, these will be high-expense-ratio, hyperactively managed funds that will underperform low-cost index funds over the long term.

When you do take out the money, you'll be paying taxes at ordinary income rates. No one knows what these rates will be a decade or more from now, but they're likely to be greater than long-term capital gains rates, which are currently capped at 15 percent.

And here's the real kicker: *Your deferred money is subject to claims of your employer's creditors in the event of bankruptcy or insolvency!*

Just how big is this risk?

Ask the former employees of Global Crossing, Adelphia Communications, Kmart, NTL, Worldcom, and Enron.

Assuming the money is really there when you need it, let's see how the numbers play out:

Let's say an employee is in the 35 percent bracket and she saved $20,000 a year for twenty years, starting in 1987.

Under Scenario #1, she paid her tax and invested the balance of $13,000 a year in a portfolio of low-cost Vanguard index funds, using the "high-risk" Vanguard portfolio described in Chapter 14.

In the beginning of 2007, she decided to take out all of her deferred assets.

At that time her portfolio was worth $781,709. She paid long-term capital gains taxes of $78,257 on the difference between her account value and her cost basis of $260,000 ($13,000 times twenty years). This leaves her with a balance of $703,453. This balance would be reduced by the taxes she would have had to pay each year on the dividends generated by her index fund holdings.

Under Scenario #2, she defers $20,000 per year, stays in her 401(k) plan, and invests in funds most similar to the "high-risk" Vanguard portfolio.

We can assume this portfolio underperformed the Vanguard portfolio by 1.25 percent a year, which is a close approximation of the difference in the average expense ratio of the Vanguard index funds and the hyperactively managed funds that were her investment options in the plan.

Her portfolio under Scenario #2 was worth $1,029,124. She paid ordinary income taxes of 35 percent, leaving her with a balance of $668,931 after tax—*less* than what she received in Scenario #2.

This analysis does not quantify the risk of bankruptcy or the possibility of sharply increased ordinary income rates at the time when you elect to no longer defer this income. However, neither of these issues should be of trivial concern.

For example, from 1932 to 1986 (a fifty-four-year period), the highest ordinary income tax rates ranged from a low of 50 percent to a high of 94 percent!

The risk of these uncertainties would seem to far outweigh the benefit that might be gained by participating in these deferred compensation plans.

The securities industry, as always, is the big winner. It brings in significant assets, takes no risks, charges outsize fees, and delivers mediocre performance.

The employer is a winner as well. It also takes no risk. It continues to transfer the burden of retirement savings from itself to its employees, at little cost, while making it appear that it is conferring a major benefit on them.

The loser, of course, is the employee. He or she bears virtually all of the cost and all of the risk. In exchange, the benefit conferred is at best marginal and at worst an unmitigated disaster.

What's the Point?

- View deferred compensation plans with skepticism.

- Keep control of your hard-earned compensation.

CHAPTER 49

Immediate Annuities: The Good Cousin

Despite generally inadequate savings rates, workers seem oddly optimistic about their retirement prospects. (Perhaps their unjustified optimism is what is keeping them from saving.)

—M. Barton Waring and Laurence B. Siegel, "Wake Up and Smell the Coffee!" *Investment Insights* (Barclays Global Investors)

Even though I've listed many problems with annuities, one kind of annuity might be an appealing option for those who want to create a steady and reliable income stream in retirement: An *immediate annuity*, or what I call the good cousin.

These annuities can be purchased by individuals at any time. A particularly opportune time to consider them may be at or near retirement, when the contributions to a 401(k), IRA, or other retirement plan end, at which point many retirees will walk away with a lump 401(k) payment . . . but then what?

Retirees assume they'll turn their investments into a machine that generates enough income to maintain their quality of life in retirement. Is that realistic?

An immediate annuity will essentially transform all or part of your retirement savings into your own individual pension by providing you with monthly checks until you die. Even if you burn through your savings from other sources, the checks will keep coming.

The beauty of this type of annuity is that the provider assumes the risk that the money will last as long as you do. You don't have to worry about outliving your assets.

Immediate annuities can be especially helpful for retirees without a pension who have some savings but only have Social Security checks for dependable income. For instance, if Social Security will cover half your expenses, you might want to consider buying an immediate annuity to cover the rest. (Retirees who expect to have ample inflation-adjusted income won't need one.)

Since you can count on monthly income with an immediate annuity, you can afford to invest your other assets more aggressively. So if you're a conservative investor and don't want to worry about the stock market's tantrums, holding an immediate annuity along with your stock portfolio greatly reduces the possibility of running out of money before life runs out on you.

One study found that an investor with a conservative portfolio (20 percent stocks, 50 percent bonds, and 30 percent cash, with no immediate annuity) had a significantly greater possibility of running out of money at a 4.5 percent withdrawal rate after twenty-five or thirty years than an investor who purchased an immediate annuity with either 25 or 50 percent of her portfolio.

Immediate annuities have other benefits: Depending on the way you fund it, most of the income you receive from an immediate annuity purchased with after-tax money is tax free. And, in many states, the cash value of an immediate annuity cannot be attached by creditors, thereby providing asset protection.

But immediate annuities aren't popular for a couple of reasons. First, advisors and others who depend on commissions don't push them because they can make far more money peddling exotic equity indexed annuities and variable annuities, which are dreadful investments. Also, some retirees are terrified of buying one and then dying soon after.

The insurance industry addressed the "premature death" fear long ago by offering immediate annuities that don't vanish when you die. For many married couples, it might make sense to buy a "joint-and-survivor option," which guarantees that the checks keep coming even after the first spouse dies. There's also the "life with period certain" option, which lasts for a person's life or specified number of years, such as ten or fifteen, whichever is longer.

Ideally, companies should offer their retirees the chance to sink some or all of their 401(k) money into an inexpensive immediate annuity that the employer manages. When the employer oversees it, the costs can be kept much lower than an annuity from a commercial provider. By one estimate, only about one in five employers offers immediate annuities to their departing 401(k) workers, and not all of these are the low-cost variety.

I'm not suggesting that immediate annuities are suitable for everyone. There are some downsides. They don't offer the best returns. (You could probably do better with a properly allocated low-cost index fund portfolio.) And because you're receiving a fixed amount, most immediate annuities won't protect you from inflation, which could erode your purchasing power significantly. However, Vanguard offers a low-cost immediate annuity that does adjust for inflation, which may be worthy of consideration.

Also, distributions to those under 59½ may be subject to a 10 percent tax penalty.

Finally, an immediate annuity is a permanent decision—you can't revoke it. So it is important to keep a portion of your portfolio in liquid investments.

These disadvantages are the trade-off for the security of a monthly check for the rest of your life—and beyond, depending on the type of immediate annuity you select.

If you are considering the purchase of an immediate annuity, you should determine whether it is best to do so with nonqualified (after-tax) money, or with tax-deferred assets rolled over from an IRA, a Roth IRA, or another retirement plan. Each of these options has tax consequences, so be sure to check with your tax advisor before making a final decision.

If you're shopping for an immediate annuity, check with the traditional low-cost providers: TIAA-CREF, Vanguard, Fidelity, or Charles Schwab. Another excellent resource is ImmediateAnnuities.com.

What's the Point?

- Consider a low-cost immediate annuity as a way to ensure that your retirement savings last as long as you do.

CHAPTER 50

Reaping Your
Retirement Benefits

As thou hast sown, so shalt thou reap.
—Pinarius

Taking out your retirement benefits, and postretirement investing, is an important and complex subject that is beyond the scope of this book.

Among the many issues for retirees to consider are the following:

- The requirements for withdrawing money from IRA accounts;

- When you should start claiming Social Security benefits;

- How those who still have pension benefits should structure those benefits;

- How to invest your excess retirement assets; and

- Whether and how to use your home as a source of retirement funds.

In Chapter 53, I have listed some resources that you will find useful for learning more about these important issues.

What's the Point?

- You need to be aware of postretirement issues.

PART SEVEN

The Closing Argument

CHAPTER 51

A Plea for Change

What your mind can conceive and believe, it can achieve.
—Napoleon Hill

Everyone should be given the opportunity to have a secure retirement.

The current retirement system benefits brokerage firms, brokers, pension consultants, insurance companies, insurance agents, the mutual fund industry, and employers.

Employees get the short end of the stick. This must be changed.

How hard would it be to fix this broken system?

Not very . . .

The following simple legislative changes would go a long way to help:

1. Require all 401(k), 403(b), and 457(b) plans to offer an array of Target Retirement Funds *and* a broad range of low-cost index funds or ETFs, similar to those in the federal employees' Thrift Savings Plan. The mutual funds in the Target Retirement Funds would primarily consist of low-cost index funds.

2. Require all retirement plans to retain a fully independent

advisor who has no interest in selling any product. Prohibit revenue sharing, directly or indirectly. The practice of mutual funds kicking back fees to advisors is *not* in the best interests of plan participants. It should be illegal.

3. Require employers and advisors to follow the principles in the Uniform Prudent Investor Act (UPIA). The UPIA has been adopted in forty-six states. It governs the conduct of trustees of trusts and other fiduciaries, requiring them to guide their investment decisions with sophisticated risk-return analysis. It emphasizes portfolio diversification and requires trustees to avoid fees, transaction costs, and other expenses that aren't justified by the realistic objectives of the trust's investment program. Finally, it prohibits "self-dealing" by fiduciaries. Very few 401(k) plans, and even fewer 403(b) and 457(b) plans, meet this standard. But companies who provide these plans—and their advisors—should be fiduciaries to their employees, who rely on their integrity and competence.

4. Require full disclosure of *all* plan expenses on an annual basis on a standard form adopted and approved by the Department of Labor.

    This form would be drafted to single out plans with excessive costs. You can be assured that plan administrators would quickly find a way to reduce these costs—or they might find themselves defending their conduct in court.

That's it.

If this legislation went through, you could trash the "cheat sheet" I've provided in Chapter 24. You wouldn't need it.

A retirement system with these simple reforms would actually *benefit* employees.

What a refreshing concept!

What's the Point?

- Some very simple legislative changes would fix a seriously broken retirement system. All that is required is the political will.

CHAPTER 52

The Journey's End

*If all difficulties were known at the outset of a long
journey, most of us would never start out at all.*
—Dan Rather

You now have the tools to invest intelligently for your retirement. This is a just reward for your diligence.

Smart Investing is very simple: Focus on your asset allocation (Appendix A). Invest in a broadly diversified portfolio of low-cost index funds or ETFs (Chapter 14). Avoid nearly all annuities and expensive, hyperactively managed funds.

Your goal is to capture market returns. They are superior returns, based on all historical data. They are yours for the taking.

Here is a final, cautionary—and sure to be controversial—note:

I agree with most advisors who believe the corporate match of a 401(k) and 403(b) plan is too good to pass up. Investors *probably* should contribute to these plans—at least the minimum amount necessary to obtain the maximum employer match. However, I'm more concerned than most about future developments that could make *any* investment in retirement plans a bad choice.

I don't know about you, but I find the government to be pretty scary. Recent events have demonstrated that it has very broad power to have a serious impact on our rights.

The possibility of retroactive legislation that could sharply reduce, or even eliminate, the benefits of current retirement planning cannot be discounted. The ability of the government to pass retroactive tax legislation going back as much as ten years has been sanctioned by the Supreme Court, which has referred to this disturbing conduct as "customary practice."

Don't take my word for it. In its brief to the Supreme Court supporting the power of the government to take away your money retroactively, the Justice Department had this chilling observation: "The taxpayer must be prepared for such possibilities."

Are you prepared for the possibility that the government could retroactively impose a new tax on distributions from your retirement accounts? It could happen. If it does, it could seriously erode the benefits of participating in these plans.

In addition, looming darkly over your retirement planning horizon is the uncertainty of the ordinary income tax rate at your retirement. It cannot be predicted or quantified. What we do know is that by investing in a tax-deferred plan, you have surrendered your right to be taxed at the historically more favorable long-term capital gains rate.

Even if tax rates stay the same, it's by no means a foregone conclusion that your postretirement tax rate will be lower than your preretirement rate. Here are some variables that could adversely affect your tax rate:

You are likely to be single at some point in retirement. If so, your status as a single filer could put you in a higher bracket.

You may decide to work in retirement, either to supplement your income or just because you may find it satisfying to do so.

You may not have the same tax breaks in retirement that you presently have—like your deduction for mortgage payments.

When you add to these potential problems the lack of liquidity of retirement plans, the limited and often poor choice of investment options available to plan participants, and the high fees buried in these plans, you begin to question the unbridled enthusiasm of financial planners and the financial media for investing in these plans.

I fully understand the hype. These plans are great for employers, for the mutual fund and insurance industries, for brokers, and for annuity salesmen.

The question only you can answer is whether they are good for you—or whether you would be better served by investing yourself, following the basic principles I have outlined.

What's the Point?

- Investing in tax-deferred plans is not the "no-brainer" that it is generally made out to be.

CHAPTER 53

Who Says So?

By three methods we may learn wisdom: First, by reflection,
which is noblest; second, by imitation, which is easiest;
and third by experience, which is the bitterest.

—Confucius

I make a lot of bold statements in this book concerning the standard
fare served up in retirement plans by the securities and insurance
industries and company sponsors. You have every right to put me to
the test of proving that there is ample authority for these views.

Among academics and others who have spent their lives studying
the capital markets and publishing their findings in peer-reviewed
journals, my statements are generally regarded as being supported by
irrefutable evidence.

Unfortunately, this evidence is buried under an avalanche of misleading advertising, intended to obscure the facts and keep employees
who are planning for their retirement distracted and confused.

This makes perfect sense: The less you know, the more likely you
are to fall in line and to continue to select hyperactively managed,
underperforming funds or sinfully expensive annuities.

You can almost *see* the flow of dollars leaving your pockets and
fattening the coffers of mutual fund families, brokers, and insurance
companies while your employer sits on the sidelines, complicit in this

mess and happy to be rid of the costs and the risks associated with traditional pension plans.

Before you can revolt and demand retirement plans that are in *your* best interest, you need to have the ammunition to load your weapons.

This bibliography is the ammunition. Take a look at it. If it persuades you, get ready to aim—and fire away!

(Note: Website addresses were current as of November 2007.)

Chapter 1: The Amazing Story of Wan Ba-shi

- "Wan Ba-shi" means "perform magic tricks" in the traditional Chinese transliteration, which is still used in Taiwan and Singapore. However, in the Pinyin transliteration, the name would be spelled "Wan Ba Xi." This spelling would be more familiar to readers who have origins in mainland China.

Chapter 2: Small Change Can Break the Bank

- Vanguard, the low-cost leader in index funds, has some useful information about costs and returns on its website. See https://personal.vanguard.com/VGApp/hnw/planningeducation/general/PEdGPFinStrtHighCostReturnsContent.jsp and https://personal.vanguard.com/VGApp/hnw/planningeducation/education/PEdIEMFBasicsActMgmtIndxContent.jsp.

- See Eric E. Haas's study *Mutual Fund Expense Ratios: How High Is Too High?* He notes that: "[A]ll else being equal, a fund with lower expenses must have higher performance than a similar fund with higher expenses." See www.altruistfa.com/Haas%20Expense%20Ratio%20Study%20working%20paper.pdf.

- The Division of Investment Management of the Securities and Exchange Commission, in its "Report on Mutual Fund Fees and

Expenses," found that "[I]ndex funds and funds that are available only to institutional investors generally have lower expense ratios than other types of funds." See www.sec.gov/news/studies/feestudy .htm#item14.

- Reams of articles demonstrate that high expense ratios reduce returns. Well-known investor advocate Errold F. Moody Jr. has compiled an excellent selection of these studies. See www.efmoody.com/ investments/fundexpenses.html.

- Professor William Sharpe, a professor of finance at Stanford University and a Nobel Laureate in Economics, summarized the importance of fees in an interview as follows: "The average dollar in an active fund will net of costs underperform the average dollar in an index fund." See www.ifa.com/sharpe.asp.

Chapter 3: Passive Is Aggressive

- For an excellent article on expense ratios, which discusses the difference in the average expense ratios of actively managed funds and index funds, see "Expense Ratios" by Bill Barker, available at www .fool.com/school/mutualfunds/costs/ratios.htm.

- The complete transcript of Rex Sinquefield's opening statement in his debate with Donald Yacktman at the Schwab Institutional Conference in San Francisco, October 12, 1995, is available at www.dfaus .com/library/articles/active_vs_passive.

I highly recommend reading this transcript. It is a classic.

- One study looked at over 23,000 funds in the Morningstar database over an eleven-year period. It found that an average of only 14 percent of top performing funds were able to repeat that performance in the following year. Details of this study can be found at www.ifa .com/12steps/step5.

■ On December 10, 2002, CNN's *Money* reported that "Bill Miller has a track record that any fund manager would kill for—he's on pace to beat the S&P 500 for a record 12th year in a row. No other fund in the history of the $6.2 trillion business has accomplished such a feat." See http://money.cnn.com/2002/12/09/funds/q_funds_leggmason/ index.htm. Personally, I think the story missed the real headline. What is really newsworthy is the fact that no other fund "has accomplished such a feat."

■ A study comparing the performance of small-cap active funds versus the Vanguard Small Cap Index Fund over various time periods found the index fund almost always outperformed. See "Active vs. Passive Management for Small Cap Funds" by Jim Wiandt, March 19, 2001, at www.indexfunds.com/archives/articles/wiandt_jim_20010319 _active_vs_passive_management_for_small_cap_funds.php.

■ The data supporting the high failure rate of mutual funds can be found at www2.standardandpoors.com/spf/pdf/index/SPIVA_2007 _q1.pdf.

■ The data supporting the wisdom of investing in index funds and not trying to "beat the markets" with hyperactively managed funds is so extensive and overwhelming that just listing it could fill up a book.

• An excellent place to start is the stellar website of Index Funds Advisors (with whom I am affiliated), www.ifa.com. Under the "library" menu, you'll find over 600 articles that discuss every aspect of this issue, together with an extensive selection of videos and quotes from Nobel laureates, famous academics, and many others.

- To keep up with timely index happenings, visit IndexUniverse .com, which provides comprehensive coverage of index funds and Exchange Traded Funds. At the site, you can also read the *Journal of Indexes*, which contains articles by leading indexing experts.

- There are a number of excellent books that delve deeply into this subject. The following is my selection of some that you might find particularly helpful:

A Random Walk Down Wall Street by Burton Malkiel (W. W. Norton, 9th ed., 2007).

Index Funds: The 12-Step Program for Active Investors by Mark T. Hebner (IFA Publishing, 2005).

Bogle on Mutual Funds by John C. Bogle (McGraw-Hill, 1993).

The Four Pillars of Investing by William Bernstein (McGraw-Hill, 2002).

The Only Guide to a Winning Investment Strategy You'll Ever Need by Larry Swedroe (St. Martin's Press, 2005).

Unconventional Success: A Fundamental Approach to Personal Investment by David F. Swensen (Free Press, 2005).

The Little Book of Common Sense Investing: The Only Way to Guarantee Your Fair Share of Stock Market Returns (Little Book Big Profits) by John C. Bogle (Wiley, 2007).

■ In *The Smartest Investment Book You'll Ever Read* (Perigee Books, 2006), I discussed in detail the extensive studies supporting index and passive investing and provided readers with model portfolios they could implement without using any broker or advisor.

- In "Will Active Mutual Funds Continue to Underperform the Market in the Future?" by John C. Bogle, the founder of Vanguard, Mr. Bogle concludes that "it is likely that in the future a given index fund will generate net long-term performance superior to most similarly invested actively-managed mutual funds. This is true for both stock and bond index funds." See www.ifa.com/archives/articles/bogle _john_1999_will_active_mutual_funds_continue_to_underperform _the_market_in_the_future.asp.

- For an excellent article on the distortions in the returns reported by actively managed funds caused by "survivorship bias," see "Survivorship Bias" by Larry Swedroe. Mr. Swedroe notes: "Funds that have poor performance are made to disappear, most often by the fund sponsor merging a poorly performing fund into a better performing one. Unfortunately for investors, only the performance reporting disappears, not the poor returns."
  The article is available at www.indexfunds.com/articles/20010413 _survivorship_com_act_LS.htm.

- Data on the performance of the Legg Mason Value Trust Mutual Fund was obtained from Yahoo! Finance, available at http://finance .yahoo.com/q/pm?s=LMVTX.

- For an article on the current woes of Bill Miller, see "Investing Legend Bill Miller Hits Rocky Patch at Legg Mason Value Trust" by Danielle Kost. It is available at www.iht.com/articles/2007/04/01/ bloomberg/bxmiller.php?page=1.

Chapter 4: A Simple Strategy for Superior Returns
- The study concerning the poor performance of pension plan managers is reported in *Index Funds: The 12-Step Program for Active Investors* by Mark T. Hebner (IFA Publishing, 2005), on page 62.

- The study showing the dismal record of 1,446 mutual funds when measured against the S&P 500 index was cited in Jeff Brown's "On Personal Finance: Beating Index Funds Takes Rare Luck or Genius," TwinCities.com. See www.ifa.com/Media/Images/PDF%20files/BeatingIndexesarehardtodo10-12-04.pdf.

- Standard & Poor's Index Versus Active (SPIVA) is the name of the quarterly report card that compares the performances of indexes versus actively managed mutual funds. For several years of data, see www2.standardandpoors.com/portal/site/sp/en/us/page.hottopic/indices_spiva/3,1,1,0,0,0,0,0,0,0,0,0,2,0,0,0.html.

- William F. Sharpe, Nobel Laureate in Economics, explores the relationship between the higher costs of actively managed funds and their underperformance when compared to comparable index funds in "The Arithmetic of Active Management," 1991. See www.stanford.edu/~wfsharpe/art/active/active.htm.

Chapter 5: Just Because It Quacks, It May Not Be a Duck!

- The curious behavior of investors who ignore the benefits of purchasing the lowest-cost index funds is explored in a study titled "The Index Fund Rationality Paradox" by Michael Boldin and Gjergji Cici. See www.fma.org/SLC/Papers/IFunds3e_mdb_.pdf.

Chapter 6: "Hot" Advice Can Give Cold Comfort

- Lynn O'Shaughnessy reported on the inability of pundits to make accurate stock predictions, including those made by *Fortune* magazine, in "Let's Look Back at How Wrong Experts Were in Their Predictions," *San Diego Union-Tribune*, January 10, 2006. See www.signonsandiego.com/news/business/shaughnessy/20060115-9999-1b15lynn.html.

- The study on market-timing newsletters, "Market Timing Ability and Volatility Implied in Investment Newsletters' Asset Allocation Recommendations" (February 1995), was performed by two researchers at Duke University and the University of Utah, John R. Graham and Campbell R. Harvey. See http://ssrn.com/abstract=6006, or DOI: 10.2139/ssrn.6006.

Chapter 7: "Hot" Funds . . . and Other Fables

- In "Morningstar Mutual Fund Ratings Redux," Matthew R. Morey and Aron Gottesman concluded that higher-rated Morningstar funds outperformed lower-rated ones. This conclusion was at odds with prior studies. However, a review of the study's data indicates that the returns of index funds beat the returns of all categories of the Morningstar ranked funds that were the subject of the study, with few exceptions. See http://webpage.pace.edu/mmorey/publicationspdf/redux.pdf.

- The study of the performance of funds selected by Morningstar and other financial publications for their 401(k) plans is Ravi Agrawal's "Active vs. Passive Investing: A Research Review," April 2004. This article is no longer available online.

- Lipper Analytical Services, a highly respected mutual fund data firm, found that in the four-year period from 1990 to 1993, a majority of the mutual funds that received the 5-star Morningstar ranking underperformed the mutual fund averages in the ensuing year. See "Selling the Future: Concerns about the Misuse of Mutual Fund Rating," May 16, 1994, referred to and discussed at www.indexfunds5.com/step5page3.php.

Chapter 8: Don't Confuse Activity with Progress

- Dalbar Inc., a financial services consulting firm, issues a report every year called *Quantitative Analysis of Investor Behavior*. The report looks at the returns that investors actually realize, as well as the investor behavior that produces those returns. The report is expensive, but you can see a snapshot at www.dalbar.com/content/showpage.asp?page=is1.

- Jason Zweig reached the same conclusions in "What Fund Investors Really Need to Know," *Money* magazine, vol. 31, no. 6 (June 2002). See www.intelligenthedgefundinvesting.com/pubs/rb-jz.pdf.

Chapter 9: Risky Behavior

- The historic stock and bond market data comes from Ibbotson Associates. Its charts illustrate how the value of a dollar bill has grown over the decades in such investment categories as large-cap stocks and small-cap stocks. This data is not available online.

Chapter 10: When Bigger Isn't Better

- You can find the standard deviations of many mutual funds by visiting the website of Morningstar (www.morningstar.com), which provides analysis of stocks and mutual funds. Much of the website's content is free.

- To learn more about computing the standard deviation of your portfolio, see http://ezinearticles.com/?Using-Standard-Deviation-and -the-Sharpe-Ratio:-Tools-of-the-Pros&id=78770.

Chapter 11: Lose the Empty Calories

- The benefits of broad asset class diversification can be traced to Harry Markowitz, joint winner of the Nobel Prize in Economics in 1990. In 1952, Mr. Markowitz wrote the seminal paper "Portfolio Selection." He is the author of *Portfolio Selection: Efficient Diversification of Investments* (Wiley, 1991). This book is considered to be an investment classic and is the foundation for what is commonly known as "Modern Portfolio Theory."

Chapter 12: The Simplest Way to Beat the "Pros"

■ In *The Smartest Investment Book You'll Ever Read* (Perigee Books, 2006), I discuss in detail the reasons why the vast majority of investors would achieve superior returns by following the basic recommendations in this chapter. You should also carefully review the risks and returns of my recommended portfolios in Appendix B.

Chapter 13: Your Biggest Investment Decision Takes Only Fifteen Minutes

■ The importance of asset allocation was studied by Gary P. Brinson, L. Randolph Hood, and Gilbert L. Beebower in "Determinants of Portfolio Performance," *Financial Analysts Journal*, vol. 42, no. 4 (July–August 1986). A follow-up study, also published in *Financial Analysts Journal*, was written by Gary P. Brinson, Brian D. Singer, and Gilbert L. Beebower, "Determinants of Portfolio Performance II: An Update," vol. 47, no. 3 (May–June 1991).

■ Two more researchers, Roger G. Ibbotson of Yale University and Paul D. Kaplan of Morningstar, explored similar territory with their study "Does Asset Allocation Policy Explain 40, 90, 100 Percent of Performance?" See http://papers.ssrn.com/sol3/papers.cfm?abstract _id=279096.

■ An excellent summary of the many studies on this subject can be found in William E. O'Reilly and James L. Chandler Jr.'s "Asset Allocation Revisited," in *Journal of Financial Planning*, January 2000. See www.fpanet.org/journal/articles/2000_Issues/jfp0100-art13.cfm.

Chapter 14: Simple Investing Is Smart Investing

- For information on Vanguard Funds, see www.vanguard.com.

- For information on Fidelity Funds, see www.fidelity.com.

- For information on T. Rowe Price Funds, see www.troweprice.com.

Chapter 15: DFA's Way (or the Highway)

- *Fortune* magazine summarizes the appeal of DFA funds in "How the Really Smart Money Invests," July 6, 1998. See http:// web.archive.org/web/20001218023000/library.northernlight.com/ SG19990714120006317.html?cb=13&sc=0.

- Dalbar Inc. periodically publishes studies of investor behavior titled "Extract of Quantitative Analysis of Investor Behavior." You can view a summary at http://dalbar.com/content/showpage .asp?page=2003071601.

- The Morningstar study is titled "Indexing Goes Hollywood," by Don Phillips. It is available at www.ifa.com/Media/Images/ PDF%20files/Morningstar-IndexingGoesHollywood.pdf.
This study also sets forth the difference in the returns actually achieved by investors in DFA funds and investors in all no-load mutual funds.

- The *Money* magazine article is titled "What Fund Investors Really Need to Know" by Jason Zweig, June 2002. It is available at www.ifa.com/Library/Support/Articles/Popular/ZweigWhatFund InvestorsReallyNeedtoKnow.pdf.

- The academic research of Eugene Fama and Kenneth French can be found in the following articles, among many others:
"The Cross-Section of Expected Stock Returns" by Eugene F. Fama

and Kenneth R. French, *Journal of Finance*, June 1992, available at www
.ifa.com/Media/Images/PDF%20files/The%20Cross-Section%20of
%20Expected%20Stock%20Returns.pdf.

"Characteristics, Covariances and Average Returns: 1929–1997" by
James L. Davis, Eugene F. Fama, and Kenneth R. French, available at
www.ifa.com/Media/Images/fama%2029-97.pdf.

- DFA's passive investment strategy was compared to Vanguard's
index funds in a study by Duke University's Edward Tower and
Cheng-Ying Yang. The study, "DFA Versus Vanguard: Has DFA Outperformed Vanguard by Enough to Justify Its Advisor Fees?" July 30,
2007, found that from 1999 to 2006, "[B]efore style adjustment, DFA
outperformed Vanguard by 8.2 percent per year." The study also found
that "[t]he DFA portfolio outperformed Vanguard's style-mimicking
portfolio by 2.4% per year." The study is available at www.econ.duke
.edu/Papers/PDF/Vanguard_Versus_DFA_30%20july_2007.pdf.

- In January 2003, Harvard Business School published an independent case study of DFA, by Randolph B. Cohen. You can purchase this
study at http://harvardbusinessonline.hbsp.harvard.edu/b01/en/
common/item_detail.jhtml?id=203026.

- Information about the West Virginia 529 Plan that offers DFA
funds may be found at www.smart529select.com/servlet/Satellite
?pagename=HI/Page/529Select_HomePage&cid=1093916353727&nt
_page_id=1093916353727&noindex=true.

Chapter 16: Keep Your Balance by Rebalancing

- Many formulas are used to determine when rebalancing is
required. A common one holds that you should rebalance when an
asset class moves (i) an absolute 5 percent, or (ii) 25 percent from its
original allocation percentage, whichever comes first.

- William J. Bernstein wrote an essay on rebalancing aimed at more sophisticated investors. See www.efficientfrontier.com/ef/100/rebal100.htm.

- For an extensive analysis of the pros and cons of rebalancing, see "Risk, Return and Rebalancing" by Patrick J. Collins and Josh Stampfli, at www.schultzcollins.com/files/Risk_Reward_and_Rebalancing.pdf.

- In "Portfolio Rebalancing," Robert A. Dennis notes that "most studies have shown that a disciplined rebalancing program does reduce risk and may improve performance over time." See www.mass.gov/perac/bulletins/Rebalancing.pdf.

- For information on Vanguard's Target Retirement Funds, see https://personal.vanguard.com/VGApp/hnw/content/Funds/FundsVanguardFundsTargetQandAJSP.jsp.

Chapter 17: Can You Feel Guilty Without a Conscience?

- Ted Benna's recollection of his first 401(k) plan is at www.malvern401k.net/about/historyof401k.html.

- For another take on the 401(k) plan's beginnings, see *History of 401(k) Plans: An Update*, available at www.ebri.org/pdf/publications/facts/0205fact.a.pdf.

- Extensive data supporting the decline of defined benefit plans and the commensurate rise in the number of 401(k) plans can be found at the nonpartisan Employee Benefit Research Institute's website. See www.ebri.org/pdf/publications/facts/0607fact.pdf.

Chapter 18: Knowledge Is Power

- In "Defined Benefit Pensions, Conflicts of Interest Involving High

Risk or Terminated Plans Pose Enforcement Challenges," the U.S. Government Accountability Office (GAO) found 13 out of 24 pension consultants failed to disclose significant conflicts of interest. The GAO determined that these consultants had over $4.5 trillion under management. The pension plans that relied on these consultants generated returns that were generally 1.3 percent lower than others. See www .gao.gov/new.items/d07703.pdf.

■ For a history of revenue sharing, see "Revenue Sharing in the 401(k) Marketplace: 'Whose Money Is It?'" prepared by the McHenry Consulting Group. Among other cogent observations, this study found that "[m]ost plan sponsors and participants don't understand fees from the investment community. It is clear to us that they don't know how much they are paying their providers." See www.plantools .com/pdfs/RevenueSharingReport_9_01.pdf.

Chapter 19: So Many Fees, So Little Time

■ In March 2007 the U.S. House of Representatives' Committee on Education and Labor held a hearing on hidden 401(k) fees. The witnesses painted a devastating picture of the financial industry feasting on the spoils of workplace plans. Stephen Butler, president of Pension Dynamics Corporation, testified that excessive fees over the past twenty years have reduced worker account balances by an average of 15 percent. See www.house.gov/apps/list/speech/edlabor_dem/ rel0306072.html.

■ The U.S. Senate Special Committee on Aging held another hearing on the subject in October 2007. See "Hidden 401(k) Fees: How Disclosure Can Increase Retirement Security," at http://aging.senate .gov/hearing_detail.cfm?id=285919&.

- For another overview on the dismal state of the nation's 401(k) plans, read M. Barton Waring and Laurence B. Siegel's "Wake Up and Smell the Coffee! DC Plans Aren't Working: Here's How to Fix Them" in the June 2006 issue of *The Investment Research Journal* from Barclays Global Investors. See http://benefitslink.com/links/20060807-045920.html.

- In an angle that's rarely examined, the *Washington Post* reported that surveys and research suggest that African Americans participate in retirement accounts at lower levels than whites and don't invest as much in stocks. Charles Schwab and Ariel Mutual Funds estimated that four out of ten African Americans with household incomes of at least $50,000 have no money invested in stocks. That's compared to one-quarter of white Americans. See www.washingtonpost.com/wp-dyn/content/article/2007/10/13/AR2007101300073.html.

- For a compelling indictment of 401(k) plans, see "Riding for a Fall: The 401(k) Is Likely to Turn Out to Be a Defined-Chaos Retirement Plan" by William Bernstein, in the November 26, 2001, issue of *Barron's*. See www.efficientfrontier.com/ef/102/401.htm.

Here's an excerpt (warning: this may keep you up at night!):

Given low equity returns, high expenses, and poor planning, it is likely that most 401(k) investors will obtain near-zero real returns in the coming decades. Further, a substantial minority will have disastrous results. Only a lucky few will save enough and obtain the 4 percent to 8 percent real returns necessary for a comfortable retirement (that is, aside from their bosses, who were smart enough to retain their traditional defined-benefit plans). When the boomers retire between 2010 and 2030, most will find the cupboard bare. The inevitable government bailout will make the savings and loan resolution of the last decade look like lunch at Taco Bell.

Mr. Bernstein is generally regarded as one of the most astute financial minds of our time. His views should be a source of grave concern to all investors in these plans.

■ In written testimony before the Committee on Education and Labor, U.S. House of Representatives, Stephen J. Butler, president of Pension Dynamics Corporation, commented on the profitability of the mutual fund industry: "According to *Forbes* magazine, the mutual fund industry is the world's most profitable as it earns a consistent 30 percent pretax profit." Mr. Butler further noted that profits on 401(k) accounts "might be as high as 94 percent." See http://edworkforce .house.gov/testimony/030607StephenButlertestimony.pdf.

Chapter 20: Company Stock: The Nail in the 401(k) Coffin

■ Ray Martin's "401(k) Advice: What to Do with Company Stock" discusses the problem of holding company stock in 401(k) plans. See www.cbsnews.com/stories/2002/05/08/earlyshow/contributors/ raymartin/main508368.shtml.

■ In an article titled "Company Stock, Market Rationality, and Legal Reform" by Shlomo Benartzi, Richard H. Thaler, Stephen P. Utkus, and Cass R. Sunstein, the authors stated that "some eleven million participants in US defined contribution plans have over 20% of their account balance invested in company stock. Within this group, some five million have over 60% of their account concentrated in employer stock. Many large US firms encourage this practice by making their own 'matching' or other contribution in the form of company stock." This study is available at www.law.uchicago.edu/Lawecon/WkngPprs _201-25/218-crs-stock.pdf.

■ Jack L. VanDerhei's testimony before the House Education and Workforce Committee's Subcommittee on Employer-Employee Relations on February 13, 2002 ("The Role of Company Stock in 401(k) Plans") gives an exhaustive analysis of the role of company stock in 401(k) plans, including a discussion of Enron. See www.ebri.org/pdf/ publications/testimony/t133.pdf.

- An excellent discussion of this issue can be found in Alicia H. Munnell and Annika Sundén's article "401(k)s and Company Stock: How Can We Encourage Diversification?" The authors accurately note that "the evidence suggests that most participants are not sophisticated investors; they underestimate the risk of investing in company stock and tend to buy what they know." See www .bc.edu/centers/crr/issues/ib_9.pdf.

- For articles about lawsuits filed against companies whose company stock is included in 401(k) plans, see www.401khelpcenter.com/ 401k/meigs_company_stock.html; www.401khelpcenter.com/401k/ meigs_classaction_summary_062005.html; www.reish.com/publica tions/article_detail.cfm?ARTICLEID=406; and www.401khelpcenter .com/press_2007/pr_wolfpopper_110607.html.

Chapter 21: If It's Broken, Fix It!

- The data in this chapter was derived from a nonpublished, private study called "Yield Disparity" by Brooks Hamilton & Partners, employee benefit consultants. I am grateful to Brooks Hamilton for providing me with a copy of this enlightening study.

As a consequence of the "yield disparity" and other issues with retirement plans, the study concludes that "many (perhaps most) American workers will retire in despair and run out of money. About one-half of all workers are not even covered by a retirement plan, while most of the half who are save too little, too late, while achieving *paltry* lifetime investment returns."

I share these concerns.

Chapter 22: Why Fifteen Is Your Magic Number

■ The study by Barclays Global Investors is "Wake Up and Smell the Coffee! DC Plans Aren't Working: Here's How to Fix Them" by M. Barton Waring and Laurence B. Siegel. See http://benefitslink.com/links/20060807-045920.html.

■ The statistics for this chapter were taken from "401(k) Plan Asset Allocation, Account Balances, and Loan Activity in 2006," published simultaneously in the August 2007 issue of *EBRI* (Employee Benefit Research Institute) *Issue Briefs* and *ICI* (Investment Company Institute) *Perspective*. See www.ebri.org/publications/ib/index.cfm?fa=ibDisp&content_id=3838.

Chapter 23: Smart Investing in a Dumb Plan

■ The statistics for this chapter were also taken from "401(k) Plan Asset Allocation, Account Balances, and Loan Activity in 2006," cited above.

■ The investment options offered to plan participants were fully explored in Edwin J. Elton, Martin J. Gruber, and Christopher R. Blake's study "The Adequacy of Investment Choices Offered by 401(k) Plans." The authors reached this troublesome conclusion: "We find that, for 62 percent of the plans, the types of choices offered are inadequate, and that over a 20-year period this makes a difference in terminal wealth of over 300 percent." See http://pages.stern.nyu.edu/~eelton/working_papers/adequacy_investment_choices_offered_401k.pdf.

■ There is no doubt that the returns of 401(k) participants are adversely affected by poor investment options, poor investment selections by the participants, and default options that are far too conservative. For a discussion of these issues, see "Funds for Retirement: The 'Life-Cycle' Approach" by Vanguard Investment Counseling & Research, at https://institutional.vanguard.com/iip/pdf/life_cycle _funds.pdf.

Chapter 24: Beat a Rigged System

▪ All data was obtained from Morningstar Principia Pro as of June 2007. I identified all funds that were in the same Morningstar category as the recommended Vanguard funds. I then eliminated all funds holding less than $500 million in assets. I further eliminated funds that had an R-squared compared to the best fit index of less than 90.

For information on "R-squared," see http://help.yahoo.com/l/us/ yahoo/finance/mutual/definitions/funds-22.html.

For equity funds, I eliminated any fund that held less than 90 percent equities. I then chose those funds that had the lowest illustrated gross expense ratio. Of course, funds can and do change their expenses, investment styles, and cash holdings. Before making an investment decision based on this list, you should do some homework to be sure that nothing significant has changed that might alter your decision.

Chapter 25: Cheat the Cheaters with an IRA

▪ For a discussion of assets that should optimally be held in nontaxable and taxable accounts, see "Non-qualified Annuities in After-Tax Optimizations," by William Reichenstein, at www.ifid.ca/Conference _Material/Reichenstein_paper.pdf.

He concludes that "all individual investors except traders should have an asset-location preference. In general, they should locate stocks in taxable accounts and bonds in tax-exempt retirement accounts (that is, Roth IRAs and qualified retirement accounts)."

Chapter 26: When Cashing In Is Cashing Out

- The Hewitt Associates study was cited in Trevor Thomas's "45 Percent of Departing Workers Cash Out 401(k)s, Hewitt Finds," at www.insurancenewsnet.com/article.asp?a=top_lh&id=47661.

Chapter 27: The Trick to Transferring Company Stock

- See "Know Your NUA: If Your 401(k) Includes Your Company's Stock, a Rollover May Be a Bad Move" by Robert Powell, at www .marketwatch.com/news/story/if-you-have-company-stock/story .aspx?guid={FB94D40D-9228-4EDD-88B7-82885B654390}.

Chapter 28: Can a Fox Advise the Chickens?

- The website of BNA Tax & Accounting has an extensive analysis of the Pension Protection Act of 2006 and the role of financial advisors. See www.bna.com/tm/pension_protectionact.htm.

- An AARP article by Christopher Gearon, "The New Pension Reform Act and You: The New Law Helps Those Workers Saving for Retirement, but May Bring the Curtain Down on Employer-Funded Pensions," correctly notes that the new act is probably the death knell for defined benefit plans. See www.aarp.org/bulletin/yourmoney/ newpensionreformact.html.

Chapter 29: Beware of "Financial Professionals" Bearing Gifts

- The devastating 2007 study mentioned in this chapter, "Assessing the Costs and Benefits of Brokers in the Mutual Fund Industry" by Daniel Bergstresser and Peter Tufano of the Harvard Business School and John M. R. Chalmers of the University of Oregon, examines the performance and expenses of thousands of mutual funds. See http:// papers.ssrn.com/sol3/papers.cfm?abstract_id=616981.

Donald Moine, a financial industry consultant, commented on the study as follows: "Within weeks, the popular media will be writing articles stating that financial advisors harm clients. Jonathan Clements, one of the most popular columnists in the *Wall Street Journal*, has long contended that most people would be better off by avoiding financial advisors and just putting their money in the bank. He may now have rigorous scientific proof to back up his arguments—and many other journalists and thought-shapers are sure to join the chorus." "The Study of the Decade," by Donald Moine, available at http:// trendfollowing.com/whitepaper/The%20Study%20of%20the% 20Decade.pdf.

Chapter 30: It's So Easy, the Government Did It!

- For information about the Thrift Savings Plan, go to www.tsp.gov.

- Jane Bryant Quinn and Jim Cramer's praise comes from "Statement for the Record by the Honorable Terrence Duffy before the House Subcommittee on the Federal Workforce and Agency Organization, April 26, 2006." See www.tsp.gov/curinfo/pressrel/2006apr26 -duffytestimonyreithearing.pdf.

Mr. Cramer, who is better known for his enthusiastic endorsement of stock picking, wrote the following about this plan in a November 29, 2004, article in *New York* magazine: "There is, ironically, one way in which we could cut the costs, keep fees low, offer strict diversification, and make sure that nobody gets ripped off: Do it the federal way. That's right—the much maligned federal government, which administers the Thrift Savings Plan for all federal employees."

See http://nymag.com/nymetro/news/bizfinance/columns/bottom line/10486.

Chapter 31: Evaluating Your Own 401(k)

- The October 2007 study "The Dynamics of Lifecycle Investing in 401(k) Plans" by Olivia S. Mitchell and Takeshi Yamaguchi of the Wharton School, University of Pennsylvania, and Gary R. Mottola and

Stephen P. Utkus of the Vanguard Center for Retirement Research, examined the behavior of more than 250,000 401(k) participants who work in companies that offer Lifecycle Funds. The researchers concluded that the use of Lifecycle Funds decreases the number of 401(k) accounts that contain no stocks or strictly stocks. Younger and less-affluent workers, as well as women, selected Lifecycle Funds because of their simplicity. See http://papers.ssrn.com/sol3/papers.cfm?abstract_id=1018891.

■ In "Life-Cycle Funds," Luis M. Viceira concludes that participants in 401(k) plans would benefit significantly if these funds were the default option in these plans instead of money market funds. See www.people.hbs.edu/lviceira/Lifecycle%20funds-20070514.pdf.

Chapter 32: Lobbying for the 401(k) You Deserve

■ For more about litigation concerning revenue-sharing practices, see "On the Rise: 401(k) Plan Fee Litigation" by Sally Higgins, at www .abanet.org/health/esource/Volume3/10/higgins.html.

■ Another summary of this litigation is "Plan Sponsors Sued over 401(k) Fees: Class Actions Highlight Need for Fiduciaries to Focus on Fees Paid by Plans" by Frederick A. Brodie, Bruce A. Ericson, Peter J. Hunt, Susan P. Serota, Susan P. Greenberg, and Erin E. McCampbell. See www.pillsburylaw.com/content/portal/publications/2006/10/2006 1030152811671/Litigation%20ERISA%20Sec%20Lit%20Exec%20 Comp%20Vol%201600%201606%2010-30-06_1.pdf.

■ In "Revenue Sharing Litigation: A Threat to 401(k) Plans," Fred Reish and Bruce Ashton attempt to justify revenue-sharing payments. They contend that "these payments reduce the costs of 401(k) plans, in some cases on a dollar-for-dollar basis and in others as an unallocated subsidy. Because the payments make plans affordable to employers, particularly small and mid-sized companies, they have been one of the major factors in the popularity and growth of 401(k) plans." See www.reish.com/publications/article_detail.cfm ?ARTICLEID=704.

- 401kHelpCenter.com has a great deal of information on 401(k) revenue sharing and other workplace retirement account trends.

Chapter 33: The Neglected IRA

- For the statistics used in this chapter, see the study "The Role of IRAs in Americans' Retirement Preparedness," published in the Investment Company Institute's Research Fundamentals, vol. 15, no. 1 (January 2006), at www.ici.org/pdf/fm-v15n1.pdf.

Chapter 34: The Nuts and Bolts of IRAs

- Extensive information about IRAs can be found at www.fool .com/ira/ira.htm and www.aarp.org/money/financial_planning/ sessionseven/individual_retirement_accounts.html.

Chapter 35: Fall in Love with the Roth IRA

- The website of the National Center for Policy Analysis has an excellent summary of the reasons why a Roth IRA may be a wise choice for many employees, available at www.ncpa.org/pub/ba/ba554.

- The IRS website has helpful information on the Roth IRA, including the income limitations. It is available at www.irs.gov/ publications/p590/ch02.html.

Chapter 36: Want to Leave Your IRA to the USA?

- For more information on bequeathing your IRA, see Ed Slott's article, "Pick Your IRA Beneficiary: Protect Yourself by

Making a Will for Your IRA," June 28, 2000, at http://money.cnn
.com/2000/06/28/strategies/q_retire_slott/.

■ "An Inherited IRA" by Roy Lewis for *The Motley Fool* includes a
link to the IRS Publication 590 (the IRS publication that sets forth the
rules relating to inheriting an IRA). See www.fool.com/Taxes/2000/
taxes000804.htm.

Chapter 37: 403(b) Plans: A National Disgrace

■ An excellent resource on 403(b) shenanigans is W. Scott Simon,
an attorney, author, certified financial planner, and columnist for
Morningstar Advisor. He has written seven columns on 403(b) plans for
Morningstar. See http://morningstaradvisor.com/articles/archive.asp
?authId=500.

Simon discusses how school districts and other employers with
403(b) plans have largely abandoned their employees to annuity
peddlers. In "Fiduciary Focus: Fleecing 403(b) Plan Participants
(Part 4)," he suggests how to create a model 403(b) plan. See http://
morningstaradvisor.com/articles/doc.asp?docId=13242.

Simon concluded as follows:

The real problem here is that the great majority of assets in 403(b)
plans (which are tax shelters) are invested in high-cost fixed and variable annuities (which are tax shelters). Large insurance companies
that offer such annuities—the usual suspects—charge schoolteachers
unconscionable fees ranging from 200 to 500 basis points in exchange
for poorly performing investment products and services provided by
salespeople disguised as "financial planners." This is just about the
ultimate in fleece jobs since under that kind of investment cost structure it's nearly impossible for plan participants to accumulate much
of a nest egg.

See http://advisor.morningstar.com/articles/doc.asp?s=1&docId =12911&pgNo=1.

- 403bwise.com is a comprehensive resource for the good, the bad, and the ugly about 403(b) plans.

Chapter 38: Looking for Help in All the Wrong Places

- The *Los Angeles Times* ran Kathy M. Kristof's "Unions' Advice Is Failing Teachers" on April 25, 2006. This article detailed the backroom endorsement deals that teachers' unions and 403(b) investment providers reached. See www.latimes.com/business/la-fi -retire25apr25,0,5019831.story?coll=la-headlines-business.

- Also see "NYSUT Has It Both Ways: When It Comes to Retirement Plans, New York State United Teachers Endorses Two High-Fee 403(b) Products. However, the Union Makes Available a Low-Cost 401(k) for Its Employees" by Joel L. Frank, *The Chief-Civil Service Leader*, at www.403bwise.com/features/nysut_jlf.html.

- In October 2006 the New York attorney general announced the settlement of a complaint relating to a 403(b) annuity plan endorsed by the New York State United Teachers. The attorney general determined that ING paid the union as much as $3 million per year for the endorsement and promotion of its annuities. ING agreed to pay a whopping $30 million in restitution and to provide full disclosure to all future participants of all costs in its plans. See www.oag.state .ny.us/press/2006/oct/ING%20AOD.pdf.

- For a devastating indictment of 403(b) plans generally, see "Reasons for and Responses to the Lack of Direct Access to No-Load, Low-Expense 403(b) Plans in Many School Districts" by Michael B. Engdahl, JD, *PIABA Bar Journal*, Fall 2006.

The reference to royalties received by the National Education Association for endorsing various products is on page 42. The article is available at http://403bwise.com/pdf/engdahl_403b_schools.pdf.

Chapter 39: The Annuity Scam

▪ For an excellent discussion of annuities, see "Annuities" by Craig J. McCann, PhD, and Kaye A. Thomas, at www.slcg.com/pdf/workingpapers/Annuities.pdf.

The authors conclude: "Annuities stand out as the investment most likely to be unsuitable since in virtually every instance, the investor would have been better served by mutual funds or a portfolio of individual stocks. That variable annuities hold more than $1 trillion in assets is a testament to the powerful incentives created by the insurance industry with generous commissions and the massive fraud they engender."

▪ For information on TIAA-CREF's low-cost annuities, see www .tiaa-cref.org.

▪ Another excellent resource for low-cost annuities is Vanguard. Information about the annuities it offers may be found at https://personal.vanguard.com/us/accounttypes/retirement/ATSAnnuities OVContent.jsp.

Chapter 40: Feeding at the Annuity Trough

▪ For a technical discussion of annuities, see M. A. Milevsky and Steven E. Posner's "Option-Adjusted Equilibrium Valuation of Guaranteed Minimum Death Benefits in Variable Annuities," June 1999, working paper no. SSB 6-99, at http://ssrn.com/abstract=167728.

The authors state: "Finally, using a cross section of average insurance expense ratios (known as Mortality and Expense charges) provided by Morningstar Data—and reasonable estimates of market volatility—we conclude that in most cases the insurance industry is charging variable annuity holders approximately five to ten times the economic value of the guarantee."

Chapter 41: Variable Annuity Rip-Off

▪ The myriad problems with variable annuities are covered in "Variable Annuities #1: Tax Deferral Can Make You *Poorer*" by Craig McCann, PhD, and Dengpan Luo, PhD. The authors conclude: "It is possible—even likely—that investors buying annuities will actually end up paying more in taxes and having less after-tax wealth at retirement, because of the *harm* caused by the tax *benefit* claimed for tax-deferred annuities."

See www.slcg.com/pdf/practicenotes/annuities_-_tax_deferral.pdf.

▪ The same authors discuss the modest value of the death benefit in "Variable Annuities #2: Guaranteed Minimum Death Benefits Are Not Much Benefit." The authors conclude: "A simple GMDB [guaranteed minimum death benefit] is typically worth almost nothing since it is unlikely that a well-diversified set of sub-accounts will be worth less than the investor's net investment at the time of the investor's death."

See www.slcg.com/pdf/practicenotes/annuities_-_GMBD.pdf.

▪ The Goldman Sachs/York University study concerning the real value of the death benefit in variable annuities is by M. A. Milevsky and Steven E. Posner, "Option-Adjusted Equilibrium Valuation of Guaranteed Minimum Death Benefits in Variable Annuities," June 1999, working paper no. SSB 6-99. It is available at http://ssrn.com/abstract=167728.

Chapter 42: Equity Indexed Annuities Are Inequitable

▪ The article referred to in the opening quotation in this chapter is "An Overview of Equity-Indexed Annuities" by Craig McCann, PhD, and Dengpan Luo, PhD. See http://slcg.com/pdf/workingpapers/EIA%20Working%20Paper.pdf.

The authors conclude: "The net result of equity-indexed annuities' complex formulas and hidden costs is that they survive as the most confiscatory investments sold to retail investors."

■ The Florida Department of Financial Services has details on Florida's investigation of sales of equity indexed annuities to senior citizens at http://myfloridacfo.com/PressOffice/ViewConsumerAlert .asp?ID=2756.

Chapter 43: Divorcing an Annuity
■ Insure.com has some useful information on getting out of an annuity. See www.insure.com/articles/annuityinsurance/annuity -surrender.html.

■ FINRA (formerly the National Association of Securities Dealers) has some useful information on dumping annuities. See www.finra .org/InvestorInformation/InvestorAlerts/AnnuitiesandInsurance/ ShouldYouExchangeYourVariableAnnuity/p006045.

■ For a more technical analysis of how to determine whether exchanging one variable annuity for another adds value, see "Exchanging Variable Annuities: An Optional Test for Suitability" by M. A. Milevsky and K. Panyagometh, at www.ifid.ca/pdf_workingpapers/ WP2003AUG8.pdf.

■ For an article discussing the tax consequences of withdrawals from an annuity, see "Beware the Tax Pinch on an Annuity Payout," Kiplinger.com, available at www.kiplinger.com/features/ archives/2003/08/annuity.html.

Chapter 44: Standing Up to Goliath—and Winning!
■ For an article discussing Bruce McNutt's battle for low-cost 403(b)

options, see "Teacher's Lesson Plan Fights High Retirement Fund Fees" by John F. Wasik. It is available at http://seattletimes.nwsource .com/html/businesstechnology/2003294119_pfwasik08.html.

Chapter 45: Taking on the Sacred Cow

▪ The study referred to in this chapter is "What's in Your 403(b)? Academic Retirement Plans and the Costs of Underdiversification" by John Angus, William O. Brown, Janet Kiholm Smith, and Richard Smith. See SSRN at http://ssrn.com/abstract=733804.

This study has caused some 403(b) plans to make changes to their offerings. See "Analysis of Investments: State of Connecticut ARP and 403(b) Plan" by John Angus, PhD, and Richard Smith, PhD, at www .osc.state.ct.us/empret/reports/ClaremontFinalStudy.pdf.

As you might expect, TIAA-CREF disputes these findings in "Serious Omissions and Flawed Methodology Mar Academic Paper about Diversification in 403(b) Retirement Plans." See www.tiaa-cref.org/ about/press/about_us/releases/pdf/c39770FINAL.pdf.

▪ A study of investment choices in 401(k) plans reached similar conclusions. "The Adequacy of Investment Choices Offered by 401(k) Plans" by Edwin J. Elton, Martin J. Gruber, and Christopher R. Blake found that 47 percent of the plans studied had inadequate investment options. As a consequence, participants in these plans had 53 percent less "terminal wealth" (funds in their plans at retirement) than they would have had if their fund choices had been adequate.

Chapter 46: Help Is on the Way

▪ The new 403(b) regulations that will go into effect on January 1, 2009, are available at www.ustreas.gov/press/releases/reports/ td%2093403_checked_.pdf.

Chapter 47: Does a Better Past Mean a Better Future?

▪ An excellent resource for information about 457(b) plans is www.457bwise.com. The article by Scott Dauenhauer referred to in the quote is available at that site. See www.457bwise.com/features/planner_sd.html.

Chapter 48: Deferred Compensation Plans for Highly Compensated Employees: A Good Deal . . . for the Securities Industry!

▪ A summary of the advantages and disadvantages of deferred compensation plans can be found at www.finance.cch.com/text/c40s10d380.asp.

▪ For a list of the largest bankruptcies from 1980 to 2006, go to www.ifa.com/Book/Book_pdf/03_Stock_Pickers.pdf.

Chapter 49: Immediate Annuities: The Good Cousin

▪ For an excellent presentation of the benefits of immediate annuities, see "Making Your Money Last for a Lifetime: Why You Need to Know about Annuities," a joint project of the Actuarial Foundation and WISER, the Women's Institute for a Secure Retirement, at www .actuarialfoundation.org/consumer/Wiser_annuities.pdf.

▪ The study demonstrating how the purchase of an immediate annuity can decrease the possibility of outliving your money is "Making Retirement Income Last a Lifetime" by John Ameriks, PhD, Robert Veres, and Mark J. Warshawsky, PhD, *Journal of Financial Planning*, December 2001. It is available at www.tiaa-crefinstitute.org/research/articles/docs/120101.pdf.

Chapter 50: Reaping Your Retirement Benefits

▪ Analyzenow.com is a rich resource for retirement and postretirement planning information.

▪ There are a number of books that provide useful information about investing for retirement. The following are especially helpful:

> *The Grangaard Strategy: Invest Right During Retirement* by Paul A. Grangaard (Perigee Books, 2002).
>
> *The New Rules of Retirement: Strategies for a Secure Future* by Robert C. Carlson (Wiley, 2004).
>
> *Your Complete Retirement Planning Road Map: The Leave-Nothing-to-Chance, Worry-Free, All-Systems-Go Guide* by Ed Slott (Ballantine Books, 2006).
>
> *Retirement Income Redesigned: Master Plans for Distribution: An Adviser's Guide for Funding Boomers' Best Years* by Harold Evensky (ed.) and Deena B. Katz (ed.) (Bloomberg Press, 2006).

▪ Glenn S. Daily's "Delaying Social Security Benefits: A Real Options Available Perspective" provides some good information on the timing of Social Security payments. It is available at www .glenndaily.com/socialsecurity.htm.

▪ The Social Security Administration has information on the "break-even" point for Social Security benefits. It is available at www .ssa.gov/retire2/breakeven-example.htm.

▪ For information about the special problems affecting women and Social Security, see www.ssa.gov/pressoffice/factsheets/women.htm and www.socialsecurity.gov/women.

▪ For a study on why women take early Social Security benefits, see "Why Do Women Claim Social Security Benefits So Early?" by Alicia H. Munnell and Mauricio Soto. It is available at www .bc.edu/centers/crr/ib_35.shtml.

- In the article "Why Are Widows So Poor?" by Nadia Karam-cheva and Alicia H. Munnell, of the Center for Retirement Research at Boston College, the authors discuss a number of reasons for the sorry financial state of widows. Among the reasons noted is the drop in Social Security and pension benefits. It is available at www .bc.edu/centers/crr/issues/ib_7-9.pdf.

- An excellent resource for information on mandatory retirement withdrawals for IRAs is *Life and Death Planning for Retirement Benefits: The Essential Handbook for Estate Planners* by Natalie Choate (Ataxplan Publications, 6th ed., 2006).

- A good explanation of the IRS minimum distribution table can be found in an article titled "IRS Minimum Distributions Table" by Kay Bell, available at www.bankrate.com/brm/itax/news/20010321b .asp.

Chapter 51: A Plea for Change

- I am not suggesting that Target Retirement Funds are right for everyone. These funds move in the same direction for all participants (from aggressive to more conservative as the designated retirement date nears). This may not be appropriate for all investors because dif-ferent investors of the same age may be able to tolerate different levels of risk due to their unique personal circumstances.

By also offering an array of low-cost index funds, passively man-aged funds, or ETFs, and an online asset allocation questionnaire, participants would have the option of determining the right asset allo-cation for them and either selecting a preallocated portfolio of Target Retirement Funds consistent with that allocation or putting together a portfolio themselves that was better suited to their asset allocation requirements. W. Scott Simon discusses this issue in his article titled "Fiduciary Focus: Fleecing 403(b) Plan Participants (Part 4)," page 3.

It is available at http://morningstaradvisor.com/articles/doc.asp?s=
1&docId=13242&pgNo=0.

- The National Center for Policy Analysis noted the poor performance of 401(k) accounts and suggested that participants would be better off "by simply purchasing index funds that reflect the performance of
the market as a whole." See the article titled "401(k) Reform: Doing It the
Right Way" by Matt Moore, available at www.ncpa.org/pub/ba/ba393/.

- Altruist Financial Advisors has a good discussion of the Prudent
Investor Rule, at www.altruistfa.com/prudentinvestorrule.htm.

Chapter 52: The Journey's End
- Make no mistake about it, the government can basically do anything it wants with your money. For a historical perspective on this
issue, see *Retroactive Legislation* by Daniel R. Troy (AEI Press, 1998).

- In *Tate & Lyle v. Commissioner of Internal Revenue*, 87 F. 3d 99 (3rd
Cir. 1996), the court upheld regulations relating to interest deductions
that were retroactive for ten years.

- No less an authority than the U.S. Supreme Court has referred to
retroactive tax legislation as "customary practice." In *United States v.
Darusmont*, 449 U.S. 292, 296-297 (U.S. 1981), the Court held: "In enact-
ing general revenue statutes, Congress almost without exception has
given each such statute an effective date prior to the date of actual
enactment. . . . This 'retroactive' application apparently has been con-
fined to short and limited periods required by the practicalities of
producing national legislation. We may safely say that it is a customary
congressional practice."
President Clinton was apparently following this "customary practice" when he initiated retroactive tax increases that were signed into
law on August 10, 1993, but made retroactive to January 1, 1993.

Then Vice President Al Gore defended this retroactive tax legislation on *This Week with David Brinkley* (August 8, 1993, Program #615), stating: "All of the hoopla and waving of arms about retroactivity is all in behalf of the wealthiest 1 percent of people in this country. Those are the only people affected by retroactivity."

The position of the Justice Department, that taxpayers should be prepared for retroactive tax increases, is found in the Brief for the United States on page 20, *United States v. Carlton*, 116 S. Ct. 2018 (1994).

So much for the famous admonition of Chief Justice Marshall that "the power to tax involves the power to destroy." *McCulloch v. Maryland*, 17 U.S. 316, 431 (1819).

The government has the power to "destroy" your retirement nest egg. Taxpayers would be well advised to recognize the fact that it may use this power in the future.

- For historical tax rates, see www.irs.gov/pub/irs-soi/histaba.pdf. (It's not comforting to do so!)

Asset Allocation Questionnaire

This questionnaire will help guide you to a proper asset allocation for your retirement portfolio. This is only meant to be a guide. For each individual investor there are many factors that cannot possibly be addressed in a generic questionnaire. (This questionnaire is also available online at www.smartestinvestmentbook.com.)

Step 1: Add up all of the money that you currently have saved for retirement. This should include 401(k) plans, 403(b) plans, and all IRAs you are using to save for retirement. Write this number down here:

Current Retirement Savings _____ ....A

Step 2: What are your annual living expenses?

Annual Living Expenses _____ ....B

Step 3: At what annual rate do you expect your salary to grow for the foreseeable future?

Annual Salary Growth Rate _____ C

Step 4: How much are you contributing (in dollars) to retirement plans? Include your contributions to all retirement plans and also include any matching contributions from your employer.

Annual Retirement Contributions _____ ....D

Step 5: Ratio of Current Retirement Savings to Annual Living Expenses. Divide the amount in Step 1 by the amount in Step 2. For example, if you have $250,000 currently saved for retirement and your living expenses are $50,000, this ratio would be 5.

$$\frac{\text{Current Retirement Savings (A)}}{\text{Annual Living Expenses (B)}} = \underline{\hspace{3cm}}$$

Step 6: Figure out how many years you have until retirement. For example, if you are 55 and plan to retire at 70, you have 15 years until retirement.

Years Until Retirement = _____

Step 7: SAS. On the matrix below, find the intersection of your years to retirement (found in the far left column) and your ratio of current retirement savings to annual living expenses (found across the top). Identify the number in this cell. This is your Savings-Age Score (SAS). To continue the example, if your ratio of current retirement savings to annual living expenses was 5 and you plan to retire in 15 years, your SAS would be 30.

SAS SCORE = _____

How many years before retirement?	Ratio of current retirement savings to annual living expenses											
	<1	1–2	2–4	4–6	6–8	8–10	10–12	12–14	14–16	16–18	18–20	>20
41 to 45 years	80	78	72	60	40	28	20	12	8	4	2	0
36 to 40 years	76	74	68	57	38	27	19	11	8	4	2	0
31 to 35 years	72	71	65	54	36	25	18	11	7	4	1	0
26 to 30 years	68	67	61	51	34	24	17	10	7	3	1	0
21 to 25 years	56	55	50	42	28	20	14	8	6	3	1	0
16 to 20 years	48	47	43	36	24	17	12	7	5	2	1	0
11 to 15 years	40	39	36	30	20	14	10	6	4	2	1	0
6 to 10 years	24	24	22	18	12	8	6	4	2	1	0	0
1 to 5 years	16	16	14	12	8	6	4	2	2	1	0	0
Retired	8	8	7	6	4	3	2	1	1	0	0	0

Step 8: Ratio of Annual Retirement Contributions to Annual Living Expenses. Divide the amount in Step 4 by the amount in Step 2. For example, if you contribute $5,000 per year to IRAs and your 401(k) (the $5,000 includes your employer's matching contributions) and your annual living expenses were $50,000, this number would be 10 percent.

$$\frac{\text{Annual Retirement Contributions (D)}}{\text{Annual Living Expenses (B)}} = \underline{\hspace{2in}}$$

Step 9: GCS. On the matrix below, find the intersection of your annual salary growth rate (found in the far left column) and your ratio of annual retirement contributions to annual living expenses (found across the top). Identify the number in this cell. This is your Growth-Contribution Score (GCS).

GCS SCORE = _____

Annual growth of current salary	Ratio of annual retirement contributions to annual living expenses								
	0%	1–3%	3–5%	5–8%	8–10%	10–15%	15–20%	20–25%	>25%
8%+	15	15	14	11	8	5	4	2	2
5%–8%	14	14	13	11	7	5	4	2	1
3%–5%	14	13	12	10	7	5	3	2	1
1%–3%	13	12	11	10	6	4	3	2	1
0%–1%	11	10	9	8	5	4	3	2	1
0%	9	9	8	7	5	3	2	1	1

Step 10: RAS. Answer the following ten questions. Next to each answer for every question there is a number in parentheses. When you decide which answer is right for you, make note of the number next to the answer. Once you have finished all of the questions, you will add up these numbers. All of these numbers added together will give you your Risk Assessment Score (RAS).

1. *In addition to your long-term investments, approximately how many months of your current expenses do you have set aside in cash or money market funds for unexpected needs?*
A. 6 months... (3)
B. 4 months... (2)
C. 2 months... (1)
D. None... (0)

2. *How many years have you been investing in the stock market?*
A. None... (0)
B. Less than 1 year.. (1)
C. More than 1 year, but less than 5 years................................. (2)
D. More than 5 years, but less than 10 years .... (3)
E. 10 years or more.. (4)

3. *I consider myself to be knowledgeable about investments and financial matters.*
A. Strongly agree .... (4)
B. Agree .... (3)
C. Somewhat agree... (2)
D. Disagree .... (1)
E. Strongly disagree .... (0)

4. *How do you feel about this statement?*
I want my investments to be risk free.
Note: *Investments with no risk have little or no expected return beyond the rate of inflation.*
A. Strongly agree .... (0)
B. Agree .... (0)
C. Somewhat agree... (1)
D. Disagree .... (3)
E. Strongly disagree .... (4)

5. *I am willing to expose my investment portfolio to some degree of risk in order to increase the likelihood of higher returns.*

A. Strongly agree .... (4)

B. Agree .... (3)

C. Somewhat agree .... (2)

D. Disagree .... (0)

E. Strongly disagree .... (0)

6. *I am comfortable with a portion of my portfolio being invested internationally.*

A. Strongly agree .... (4)

B. Agree .... (3)

C. Somewhat agree .... (2)

D. Disagree .... (1)

E. Strongly disagree .... (0)

7. *When my investment portfolio declines, I begin to think about selling off some of my positions and reinvesting at some later date.*

A. Strongly agree .... (0)

B. Agree .... (1)

C. Somewhat agree .... (2)

D. Disagree .... (3)

E. Strongly disagree .... (4)

8. *Some investors hold portfolios that consist entirely of stocks. Such investors lost approximately 20 percent of their portfolios in October 1987. If you owned a risky investment that fell by 20 percent over a very short period, what would you do?*

A. Sell all the remaining investment .... (0)

B. Sell 75 percent of the remaining investment .... (0)

C. Sell 50 percent of the remaining investment .... (1)

D. Sell 25 percent of the remaining investment .... (2)

E. Hold on to the investment .... (4)

9. *What is the worst twelve-month percentage loss you would tolerate for your long-term investments, beyond which you would sell some or all of your investments?*

A. 24 percent .... (4)

B. 16 percent .... (3)

C. 12 percent .... (2)

D. 8 percent .... (1)

E. Zero; any loss is unacceptable to me .... (0)

10. *Based on $100,000 invested since 1975, the following choices show the highest twelve-month gain and the highest twelve-month loss of five different index portfolios. Which portfolio would you choose?*

Note: The portfolios with the widest range between the loss and the gain also have higher average returns.

A. Loss of $560; gain of $23,500 .... (0)

B. Loss of $5,100; gain of $31,000 .... (1)

C. Loss of $10,500; gain of $42,700 .... (2)

D. Loss of $15,700; gain of $51,600 .... (3)

E. Loss of $22,200; gain of $63,100 .... (4)

RAS SCORE = _____

Step 11: PAS (SAS + GCS + RAS). Add your Savings-Age Score (SAS), your Growth-Contribution Score (GCS), and your Risk Assessment Score (RAS). This number is your Portfolio Allocation Score (PAS). Find where your score lies in the distribution on page 207. The matrix below gives you a range for the stock portion of your allocation. Your recommended percentage allocated to stocks in most cases would be in this range. Once you choose the percent allocation to stocks, the remainder will be invested in bonds. Of the amount allocated to stocks, remember that 70 percent of that amount should be in U.S. stocks and 30 percent in international stocks.

PAS SCORE = _____

% Stocks		
PAS	Upper Boundary	Lower Boundary
80–120	90	70
70–79	80	60
60–69	70	50
50–59	60	40
40–49	50	30
30–39	40	20
20–29	30	10
10–19	20	0
0–9	10	0

APPENDIX B

Risk and Return Summary

All performance data are expressed in percentages and are hypothetical investment results over the period 1970–2009.

RISK AND RETURN SUMMARY OF
ULTRA CONSERVATIVE 6-MONTH TREASURY BILLS

	Ultra-Low Risk
Average Annual Return (Geometric)	6.51%
Annualized Standard Deviation	3.39%
Worst Single-Calendar Year	0.58%
Worst Two-Calendar-Year Period	2.54%
Worst Three-Calendar-Year Period	4.80%
Growth of $20,000 from 1970 to 2009	$248,876

CURRENT COMPOSITION OF 6-MONTH TREASURY BILLS

Fund Name	Ultra-Low Risk
Merrill Lynch U.S. 6-Month Treasury Bill Index	100%

Raw data used to create simulated index performance numbers:
Merrill Lynch U.S. 6-Month Treasury   1970–2009: actual index returns
Bill Index

RISK AND RETURN SUMMARY OF
FOUR VANGUARD/INDEX SIMULATED MODEL PORTFOLIOS

	Low Risk	Medium-Low Risk	Medium-High Risk	High Risk
Average Annual Return (Geometric)	8.67%	9.25%	9.70%	9.99%
Annualized Standard Deviation	6.84%	8.80%	11.64%	14.86%
Worst Single-Calendar Year	−3.79%	−12.63%	−21.47%	−30.32%
Worst Two-Calendar-Year Period	−0.32%	−10.28%	−19.74%	−28.69%
Worst Three-Calendar-Year Period	8.17%	−1.21%	−15.03%	−27.51%
Growth of $20,000 from 1970 to 2009	$557,041	$689,104	$810,201	$902,839

CURRENT COMPOSITION OF
FOUR VANGUARD/INDEX SIMULATED MODEL PORTFOLIOS

Fund Name	Low Risk	Medium-Low Risk	Medium-High Risk	High Risk
Vanguard Total Stock Market Index Fund	14%	28%	42%	56%
Vanguard Total International Stock Index Fund	6%	12%	18%	24%
Vanguard Total Bond Market Index Fund	80%	60%	40%	20%

Raw data used to create simulated index performance numbers:

Vanguard Total Stock Market Index
1993–2009: actual fund returns
1976–1992: (Wilshire 5000 Index − .25% per year)
1970–1975: [(.85*S&P 500 + .15*CRSP Sm. Co Index) − .25% per year]

Vanguard Total International Stock Index
1997–2009: actual fund returns
1970–1996: (MSCI EAFE Index − .35% per year)

Vanguard Total Bond Market Index
1987–2009: actual fund returns
1976–1986: (Lehman Bros. Aggregate Bond Index − .32% per year)
1970–1975: (CRSP Intermediate Term Gov't Bond Index − .32% per year)

RISK AND RETURN SUMMARY OF
FOUR FIDELITY/INDEX SIMULATED MODEL PORTFOLIOS

	Low Risk	Medium-Low Risk	Medium-High Risk	High Risk
Average Annual Return (Geometric)	8.70%	9.25%	9.67%	9.94%
Annualized Standard Deviation	6.90%	8.85%	11.65%	14.84%
Worst Single-Calendar Year	−4.68%	−13.13%	−21.57%	−30.01%
Worst Two-Calendar-Year Period	−0.53%	−10.44%	−19.86%	−28.77%
Worst Three-Calendar-Year Period	7.85%	−0.50%	−14.82%	−27.71%
Growth of $20,000 from 1970 to 2009	$562,147	$688,148	$801,434	$885,648

CURRENT COMPOSITION OF FOUR FIDELITY/INDEX SIMULATED MODEL PORTFOLIOS

Fund Name	Low Risk	Medium-Low Risk	Medium-High Risk	High Risk
Fidelity Spartan Total Market Index Fund	14%	28%	42%	56%
Fidelity Spartan International Index	6%	12%	18%	24%
Fidelity U.S. Bond Index	80%	60%	40%	20%

Raw data used to create simulated index performance numbers:

Fidelity Spartan Total Market Index	1998–2009: actual fund returns
	1976–1997: (Wilshire 5000 Index − .25% per year)
	1970–1975: [(.85*S&P 500 + .15*CRSP Sm. Co Index) − .25% per year]
Fidelity Spartan International Index	1998–2009: actual fund returns
	1970–1997: (MSCI EAFE Index − .35% per year)
Fidelity U.S. Bond Index	1991–2009: actual fund returns
	1976–1990: (Lehman Bros. Aggregate Bond Index − .32% per year)
	1970–1975: (CRSP Intermediate Term Gov't Bond Index − .32% per year)

RISK AND RETURN SUMMARY OF
FOUR T. ROWE PRICE/INDEX SIMULATED MODEL PORTFOLIOS

	20/80 Low Risk	40/60 Medium- Low Risk	60/40 Medium- High Risk	80/20 High Risk
Average Annual Return	8.60%	9.15%	9.55%	9.82%
Annualized Standard Deviation	6.86%	8.79%	11.60%	14.80%
Worst Single-Calendar Year	−3.40%	−12.25%	−21.09%	−29.94%
Worst Two-Calendar-Year Period	−0.55%	−10.53%	−20.00%	−28.97%
Worst Three-Calendar-Year Period	7.81%	−1.28%	−15.15%	−27.66%
Growth of $20,000 from 1970 to 2009	$543,156	$662,918	$769,391	$846,726

CURRENT COMPOSITION OF
FOUR T. ROWE PRICE/INDEX SIMULATED MODEL PORTFOLIOS

Fund Name	20/80 Low Risk	40/60 Medium- Low Risk	60/40 Medium- High Risk	80/20 High Risk
T. Rowe Price Total Equity Market Index	14%	28%	42%	56%
T. Rowe Price International Equity Index	6%	12%	18%	24%
T. Rowe Price U.S. Bond Index	80%	60%	40%	20%

Raw data used to create simulated index performance numbers:

T. Rowe Price Total Equity Market Index	1999–2009: actual fund returns 1976–1998: (Wilshire 5000 Index − .40% per year) 1970–1975: [(.85*S&P 500 + .15*CRSP Sm. Co Index) − .40% per year]
T. Rowe Price International Equity Index	2001–2009: actual fund returns 1970–2000: (MSCI EAFE Index − .50% per year)
T. Rowe Price U.S. Bond Index	2001–2009: actual fund returns 1976–2000: (Lehman Bros. Aggregate Bond Index − .30% per year) 1970–1975: (CRSP Intermediate Term Gov't Bond Index − .30% per year)

Acknowledgments

I benefited greatly from the views of my patient and insightful publisher, John Duff at Perigee Books.

Lynn O'Shaughnessy, an extremely talented financial journalist, worked closely with me. It is no exaggeration to say that this book could not have been written without her assistance.

Whitney Joiner, another talented journalist, provided invaluable editorial assistance, which markedly improved the clarity of my writing.

Sean Kelly of Kelly & Associates, LLC, provided financial analysis and gave an overall review and perspective of the book that made a significant contribution to the final product.

Edward S. O'Neal, PhD, an expert witness with Securities Litigation Consulting Group, gave me the benefit of his considerable financial expertise.

My literary agent, Carol Mann of the Carol Mann Agency, believed in my prior book, *The Smartest Investment Book You'll Ever Read*, and has remained a source of support and guidance.

Mark T. Hebner graciously gave me permission to use information from his stellar website, www.ifa.com.

Kevin Laughlin reviewed the manuscript and provided very helpful insights for improving it.

Publisher's Note

This publication contains the opinions and ideas of its author. It is intended to provide helpful and informative material on the subject matter covered. It is sold with the understanding that the author and publisher are not engaged in rendering professional services in the book. If the reader requires personal assistance or advice, a competent professional should be consulted.

The author and publisher specifically disclaim any responsibility for any liability, loss, or risk, personal or otherwise, which is incurred as a consequence, directly or indirectly, of the use and application of any of the contents of this book.

Trademarks: All terms mentioned in this book that are known to be or are suspected of being trademarks or service marks have been appropriately capitalized. Perigee Books cannot attest to the accuracy of this information. Use of a term in this book should not be regarded as affecting the validity of any trademark or service mark.

Legal disclaimer: This book provides general information that is intended, but not guaranteed, to be correct and up-to-date. The information is not presented as a source of tax or legal advice. You should not rely on statements or representations made within the book or by any externally referenced sources. If you need tax or legal advice upon which you intend to rely in the course of your business or legal affairs, consult a competent, independent accountant or attorney.

Index

Page numbers in **bold** indicate tables.

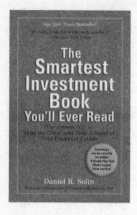

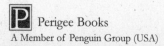
T115.0310